EDMONDS

from café . . .

great tastes

. . . to comfort

Also available:

Edmonds Food for Flatters
Edmonds Illustrated Cookbook II
Edmonds Muffins, Breads, Biscuits & Slices
Edmonds Microwave Cookbook
The New Edmonds Junior Cookbook
Edmonds for Young Cooks: Beyond the Basics

Edmonds Cooking Class

Pasta & Rice
Easy Ethnic
Barbecue
Christmas Treats
Summer Flavours
Kids' Lunchboxes & Snacks
Cakes

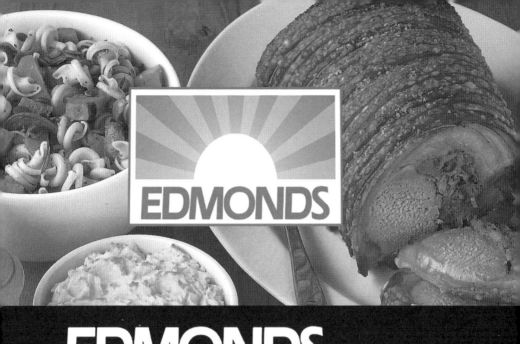

EDMONDS

from café . . .

great tastes

. . . to comfort

Hodder Moa Beckett

Acknowledgements
Most of the tableware kindly supplied by NEST of Newmarket

National Library of New Zealand Cataloguing-in-Publication Data

Lyons, Sue.
Edmonds great tastes: from café to comfort/text and food styling by Sue Lyons; photography by Bruce Benson.
Includes index.
ISBN 1-86958-957-2
1. Cookery. I. Benson, Bruce. II. Goodman Fielder N.Z. III. Title.
641.5 — dc 21

ISBN 1-86958-957-2

© 2003 Original text and photography — Goodman Fielder New Zealand Limited
The moral rights of the author have been asserted.

© 2003 Design and format — Hodder Moa Beckett Publishers Ltd

Published in 2003 by Hodder Moa Beckett Publishers Ltd,
[a member of the Hodder Headline Group]
4 Whetu Place, Mairangi Bay, Auckland, New Zealand

Reprinted 2005

Produced and designed by Hodder Moa Beckett Publishers Ltd
Text and food styling by Sue Lyons
Photography by Bruce Benson
Food styling assistant, Robyn MacDonald

Scanning by Microdot
Printed by Everbest Printing Co. Ltd in China

contents

introduction

For over 90 years Edmonds cookbooks have been part of nearly every New Zealander's recipe book collection, and an edition of the first modest *Edmonds Cookery Book*, offering economical yet tempting everyday recipes, is still in print today. Building on that great tradition, Edmonds has a growing range of cookbooks designed to capture New Zealanders' culinary imagination.

Great Tastes — From Café to Comfort continues in this tradition. It provides variations on old-time favourites, as well as new and innovative ideas utilising the very best New Zealand food and produce. This is a great selection of easy-to-prepare, tasty recipes — from ideas for hearty breakfasts and brunches; muffins, loaves and other favourites fresh from the oven; to tempting light dishes, soups and salads that are ideal for lunches or snacks. There are also traditional favourites such as roasts and chicken recipes and many new contemporary dishes, and some great vegetable accompaniments. The mouth-watering selection of desserts features traditional puddings, fruit crumbles, pies and tarts, as well as a variety of decadent little sweet treats to serve with coffee.

A section on weights, measurements and a list of useful ingredients and menu ideas completes the book. All the recipes are thoroughly tested to ensure they meet the trusted Edmonds stamp of reliability and quality — and great taste.

We hope you enjoy the recipes in this book and agree with us that they are, indeed, more 'great tastes' from the Edmonds Team.

weights and measures

New Zealand Standard metric cup and spoon measures are used in all recipes. All measurements are level.

Easy measuring — use measuring cups or jugs for liquid measures and sets of 1 cup, ½ cup, ⅓ cup and ¼ cup for dry ingredients.
Brown sugar measurements — are firmly packed so that the sugar will hold the shape of the cup when tipped out.
Eggs — No. 6 eggs are used as the standard size.

ABBREVIATIONS
l = litre
ml = millilitre
cm = centimetre
mm = millimetre
g = gram
kg = kilogram
°C = degrees Celsius

STANDARD MEASURES
1 cup = 250 millilitres
1 litre = 4 cups
1 tablespoon = 15 millilitres
1 dessertspoon = 10 millilitres
1 teaspoon = 5 millilitres
½ teaspoon = 2.5 millilitres
¼ teaspoon = 1.25 millilitres

APPROXIMATE METRIC/IMPERIAL CONVERSIONS IN COMMON COOKING USE

WEIGHT
25 g = 1 ounce
125 g = 4 ounces
225 g = 8 ounces
500 g = 1 pound
1 kg = 2¼ pounds

VOLUME
1 litre = 1¾ pints

MEASUREMENTS
1 cm = ½ inch
20 cm = 8 inches
30 cm = 12 inches

WEIGHTS AND MEASURES — APPROXIMATE EQUIVALENTS

ITEM	MEASURE	WEIGHT
breadcrumbs (fresh)	1 cup	50 g
butter	2 tablespoons	30 g
cheese (grated, firmly packed)	1 cup	100 g
cocoa	4 tablespoons	25 g
coconut	1 cup	75 g
cornflour	4 tablespoons	25 g
cream	½ pint	300 ml
dried fruit (currants, sultanas, raisins, dates)	1 cup	150–175 g
flour	1 cup	125 g
golden syrup	1 tablespoon	25 g
milk	1 cup	250 ml
oil	1 tablespoon	15 ml
rice, sago	2 tablespoons	25 g
	1 cup	200 g
salt	2 tablespoons	25 g
sugar, white	2 tablespoons	30 g
	1 cup	250 g
sugar, brown	1 cup (firmly packed)	200 g
	1 cup (loosely packed)	125–150 g
sugar, icing	1 cup	150 g
standard No. 6 egg		about 50 g

BEFORE AND AFTER EQUIVALENT MEASURES
Approximate amounts needed to give measures:
⅓ cup uncooked rice = 1 cup cooked rice
2–3 chicken pieces = 1 cup cooked chicken
100 g cheese = 1 cup grated cheese
75 g mushrooms = 1 cup sliced = ½ cup cooked
4 slices toast bread = 1 cup fresh beadcrumbs
200 g (2) potatoes = 1 cup mashed potato

OVEN CONVERSIONS
160°C = 325°F
180°C = 350°F
190°C = 375°F
200°C = 400°F

A GUIDE TO OVEN TEMPERATURES AND USE

PRODUCT	°C	°F	GAS No.	DESCRIPTION
meringues, pavlova	110–140	225–275	¼–1	slow
custards, milk puddings, shortbread, rich fruit cakes, casseroles, slow roasting	150–160	300–325	2–3	moderately slow
biscuits, large and small cakes	180–190	350–375	4–5	moderate
roasting, sponges, muffins, short pastry	190–220	375–425	5–6	moderately hot
flaky pastry, scones, browning toppings	220–230	425–450	6–8	hot
puff pastry	250–260	475–500	9–10	very hot

OVEN HINTS

Oven racks — position before turning oven on.

Oven positions
Bottom of oven — for slow cooking and low temperature cooking
Middle of oven — for moderate temperature cooking
Above middle — for quick cooking and high temperature cooking

Fan-forced ovens — refer to the manufacturer's directions as the models vary.

Preheat oven to required temperature before food preparation. Cooking temperatures and times are a guide only as ovens may vary.

useful terms and ingredients

Arborio rice is a short grain rice predominantly grown in Italy. It is used as the basis of Italian-style risotto dishes. As arborio rice cooks, the starch released from the granules thickens the sauce, giving a creamy consistency.

Bake blind To place a piece of baking paper in an unbaked pastry case, fill with dried beans or rice, and bake. This enables the pastry to bake with a flat base. Beans or rice for baking blind can be stored and re-used.

Baking powder is a mixture of cream of tartar and baking soda plus wheat fillers, which helps the baking powder to flow easily.

Baking soda is also known as bicarbonate of soda.

Basmati rice is an aromatic long grain rice with a nutty flavour. Basmati rice is used extensively in Indian cuisine.

Blanching vegetables Place vegetables in boiling water briefly until just tender. Drain in a sieve and cool under cold running water.

Coconut throughout this cookbook means desiccated unless otherwise stated. Coconut can be toasted by heating it in a frying pan over a moderate heat. Shake the pan from time to time. Remove pan from heat when coconut just starts to colour.

Cornflour is made from maize and is a starch used to thicken products such as sauces and desserts, or it can be used in some baked products.

Eggs should be at room temperature when making baked goods as this produces a product with better volume. Egg whites for making meringues and pavlovas should always be at room temperature.

Fresh breadcrumbs One toast-cut slice of Nature's Fresh bread yields ¾ cup of breadcrumbs. To make fresh breadcrumbs, break up bread and place in a food processor. Pulse to a fine crumb.

Grilled vegetables Cut vegetables into chunks or lengths. Brush all over with Rizzoli extra virgin olive oil. Place in a roasting dish under a preheated grill, turning frequently, until vegetables are golden and tender. Vegetables suitable for grilling include potato, pumpkin, kumara, onion, capsicum, courgette, carrot and asparagus.

Lemons Two main lemon types are grown in New Zealand, Meyer and Lisbon. Meyer lemons have a soft bright yellow flesh and semi-sweet flavour. They make a good garnish but do not have a lot of flavour in cooking. Lisbon lemons have a light, hard skin, a light lemon flesh and a sharper lemon taste. They should always be used in cooking where setting is required, as in condensed-milk cheesecakes, lemon honey and lemon meringue pies.

Marinate To leave meat, poultry or fish in a tenderising or flavouring liquid (the marinade) for a period of time.

Measuring All recipes in this book have been developed using standard metric measuring cups and spoons. All measurements are level. For easiest measuring use measuring cups or jugs for liquid measures and sets of 1 cup, ½ cup and ¼ cup for dry ingredients. Brown sugar measures are firmly packed so that the sugar will hold the shape of the cup when tipped out.

Melting chocolate Care is needed when melting chocolate. Intense heat will cause the chocolate to turn into an unusable lump.

On stove — place water to a level of 3 cm in a small saucepan. Bring to the boil. Sit a tight-fitting heatproof bowl over saucepan, ensuring the bowl does not touch the water. Add chocolate and stir constantly over just simmering water until chocolate has melted.

In microwave oven — place chocolate in a microwave-proof bowl. Microwave on 50% power for 30 seconds. Stir. Repeat this process until chocolate has melted.

Parmesan cheese When a recipe calls for grated parmesan cheese, avoid using pre-grated cheese as the flavour is inferior to freshly grated parmesan.

Pasta One cup of dried pasta yields approximately 2½ cups of cooked pasta. As a guideline allow:

    100 g dried pasta per serve for a main meal
    50 g dried pasta per serve for a starter
    75 g dried pasta per serve for a salad

Roasted capsicums Cut capsicums in half lengthwise. Remove core and place cut-side down on a baking tray. Bake at 200°C for 15 minutes or until skins are blistered and browned. Transfer to a bowl. Cover bowl and allow capsicums to cool. Peel off skin.

Sieve To pass through a mesh to get an even consistency.

Sift To pass dry ingredients through a mesh to remove lumps and/or foreign matter, or to mix evenly.

Stir-fry To stir and toss prepared ingredients in hot oil very quickly, resulting in moist meats and crisp vegetables.

Toasted Turkish bread Cut Quality Bakers Turkish bread into desired lengths then cut in half horizontally. Brush cut surfaces with Rizzoli extra virgin olive oil. Toast under a preheated grill.

Toasting/roasting nuts Place nuts in an ovenproof dish and cook at 180°C for 5–15 minutes, depending on the nuts, until light golden. Toss during cooking.

Toasting coconut, pinenuts, sesame seeds and pumpkin seeds Place coconut, pinenuts or seeds in a frying pan. Cook over a medium heat, stirring frequently, until light golden.

Tomato paste is concentrated tomato purée.

Tomato purée is available in cans or can be made from fresh tomatoes in a blender or food processor.

Vinaigrette Dressing Make dressing by combining all ingredients. Pour over salad and toss gently.

    ¼ cup Rizzoli extra virgin olive oil
    2 tablespoons Rizzoli balsamic vinegar
    ½ teaspoon Dijon mustard
    salt and freshly ground black pepper to season

breakfast and brunch

Wake up sluggish and need something to kick-start your day? Then try any of these delicious recipes — just the boost you need to get you going. They are nourishing, easy to prepare, and look and taste delicious. To enjoy on a lazy Sunday morning in bed with the newspaper, or after the gym before you get into the workday rush — there is something for everyone here.

chunky honey
toasted muesli

3 cups Fleming's wholegrain rolled oats
½ cup Champion Betamin wheatgerm
½ cup thread coconut
½ cup roughly chopped hazelnuts
¼ cup liquid honey
¼ cup Amco canola oil
½ cup chopped dried apricots or dried peaches

Combine oats, wheatgerm, coconut and hazelnuts in a roasting dish. Drizzle over honey and oil. Mix well. Bake at 190°C for 20 minutes or until golden, stirring every 4–5 minutes. Stir in apricots. Cool. Transfer to an airtight container. Serve with seasonal fresh fruit and/or yoghurt. (Greek yoghurt is particularly delicious served with this muesli.) **Makes 5½ cups.**

bircher muesli

70 g packet blanched almonds, chopped
½ cup chopped Brazil nuts
½ cup sunflower seeds
3 cups Fleming's rolled oats
1 teaspoon cinnamon
1 cup chopped dried apple
½ cup chopped dried apricots

Combine almonds, Brazil nuts and sunflower seeds in a roasting dish. Bake at 190°C for 5–6 minutes, turning once, until lightly toasted. Cool. Combine with remaining ingredients. Mix well. Store in an airtight container. **Makes about 5 cups (or 10 serves).**

To serve: For each serve, combine ½ cup of the dry mix with ¼ cup thick natural unsweetened yoghurt (Greek yoghurt is ideal) and ¼ cup pure orange juice. Mix well. Cover and refrigerate overnight. Serve with fresh fruit — mixed fresh berry fruit or a combination of sliced stonefruit is delicious.

porridge
with topping suggestions

Fleming's rolled oats and milk oaties are specifically designed for making perfect porridge. Kick-start your day with a healthy, satisfying bowl of porridge made from Fleming's rolled oats, topped off with one of the following. Serve with milk or, for a treat, cream.

- Drizzle with maple syrup and top with sliced banana.
- Sprinkle with brown sugar, then top with crème fraîche.
- Drizzle with liquid honey and top with sliced fresh seasonal fruit.
- Drizzle with golden syrup and top with drained canned sliced peaches. Sprinkle with cinnamon.
- Sprinkle with demerara sugar.
- Sprinkle with your favourite nuts. Try toasted almonds, walnuts or pistachios.
- For a low fat topping, serve with sliced seasonal fruit or banana and low fat yoghurt.

buttermilk hot cakes

1¼ cups buttermilk
2 tablespoons butter, melted
1 cup Champion standard grade flour
¼ teaspoon salt
¾ teaspoon Edmonds baking powder
¾ teaspoon Edmonds baking soda
1 egg
extra melted butter to cook

Combine buttermilk and butter in a jug. Sift flour, salt, baking powder and soda into a bowl. Make a well in centre of dry ingredients. Break in egg. Use a wire whisk to mix egg into surrounding flour. Add buttermilk to flour in a steady stream, whisking constantly until mixture is smooth. Heat a heavy-based frying pan or griddle over a medium heat. Brush lightly with butter. Cooking one at a time, pour in enough mixture to make a 10-cm circle. Cook for 3–4 minutes until bubbles appear on the surface. Turn with a spatula and cook for 2–3 minutes. Pile on top of each other to keep warm while cooking remaining hot cakes. **Makes 8.**

Topping Suggestions
- Sliced banana and/or hulled, halved strawberries with crème fraîche and drizzled with maple syrup.
- Grilled bacon and drizzled with maple syrup.
- Hulled, halved strawberries and fruit yoghurt.

Cook's Hint: *For a super-quick breakfast or brunch fix, try Quality Bakers Hot Cakes. Simply remove from the pack and warm according to instructions on the packet. Serve hot cakes in a stack or individually, with the topping suggestions above.*

waffles

A waffle maker is required to make waffles. They are available from most electrical appliance stores.

2 cups Champion standard grade flour
2 teaspoons Edmonds baking powder
2 tablespoons sugar
2 eggs
1 ½ cups milk
75 g butter, melted
melted butter to grease
sliced banana or strawberries to serve
whipped cream or crème fraîche to serve

Preheat waffle maker. Sift flour and baking powder into a bowl. Stir in sugar. Make a well in the centre of the dry ingredients. Break in eggs. Using a wire whisk or wooden spoon, whisk eggs into the flour. Gradually add the milk, stirring constantly. Stir in melted butter. Brush heated surface of waffle maker with melted butter. Pour half a cup of batter onto greased surface, spreading evenly with a spatula. Close lid and cook for 2–3 minutes until golden. Remove waffle and repeat with remaining batter. To serve, divide waffles into sections and arrange on serving plates with sliced fruit. Serve with whipped cream or crème fraîche. **Makes 6 waffles**.

french toast
with ricotta and banana

3 eggs
½ cup milk
2 firm ripe bananas
1 tablespoon lemon juice
3 tablespoons sugar
8 slices Quality Bakers thick-cut fruit bread
  (or Nature's Fresh toast-cut white bread)
ricotta cheese to spread
butter to grease
maple syrup to serve

Whisk together eggs and milk. Tip into a shallow dish. Peel bananas and cut into 5-mm-thick slices. Place in a bowl. Sprinkle over lemon juice and sugar. Toss to combine. Spread one side of bread slices with ricotta. Arrange pieces of banana in a single layer on 4 slices of the bread. Sandwich with remaining slices. Melt a little butter in a frying pan over a low-medium heat. Dip sandwiches into egg mixture one at a time. Cook for 3–4 minutes on each side or until golden. Cut into wedges and serve drizzled with maple syrup. **Serves 4**.

Cook's Hint: *Use fresh sliced peaches or nectarines instead of bananas.*

preserves
to serve with toasted breads

Quality Bakers selection of breads are perfect for toasting. Accompany with the following homemade spreads for a memorable breakfast.

raspberry jam

3 cups raspberries, fresh or frozen
2³/₄ cups sugar

Put the berries into a preserving pan and cook slowly until juice runs from them. Bring to the boil. Add sugar and stir until dissolved. Boil briskly for 3–5 minutes. Pour into hot, clean, dry jars. Cover with jam covers. This jam firms up after a few days storage and will keep for up to 1 year. **Makes about 2 x 350 ml jars**.

boysenberry jam

Omit raspberries and replace with boysenberries.

lemon curd

50 g butter
³/₄ cup sugar
1 cup lemon juice
2 eggs, beaten
1 teaspoon finely grated lemon zest

Melt the butter in the top of a double boiler or in a small heatproof bowl sitting over a saucepan of simmering water. Add sugar and lemon juice, stirring until sugar is dissolved. Add eggs and lemon zest. Cook over the double boiler, stirring constantly, until mixture thickens. Pour into hot, clean, dry jars. Cover with preserve covers or a lid. Refrigerated, lemon honey will keep for up to 1 month. **Makes about 2 x 250 ml jars**.

refrigerated orange, lime and ginger marmalade

1 litre freshly squeezed orange juice
finely sliced zest of 2 oranges
juice of 6 limes
2½ cups sugar
½ cup chopped crystallised ginger

Combine orange juice, orange zest and lime juice in a large saucepan. Cover pan and bring to the boil. Simmer for 1 hour. Add sugar. Boil uncovered for 30 minutes. Remove from heat. Add ginger. Cool. Transfer to clean jars or containers. Covered and refrigerated, this marmalade will keep for up to 3 months. **Makes 4 cups**.

dried apricot conserve

200 g dried apricots, quartered
1 cup water
¼ cup sugar
2 tablespoons lemon juice

Combine apricots and water in a saucepan. Bring to the boil. Reduce heat and simmer for about 20 minutes until soft. Add sugar and lemon juice and stir until sugar has dissolved. Cool. Store in a covered container in the refrigerator. **Makes 1½ cups**.

banana pastry parcels

2 sheets Ernest Adams Pre-rolled Fether Flake puff pastry
2 bananas
about ⅓ cup chocolate hazelnut spread
1 egg, beaten
icing sugar to dust

Cut each pastry sheet into 4 equal pieces. Cut bananas in half lengthwise, then cut each piece in half. Trim each piece of banana to a length of 8 cm. To make each parcel, spread about 2 teaspoons of hazelnut spread in an 8-cm-long log diagonally across one corner of the pastry, leaving a 2-cm border of pastry. Place a piece of banana cut-side down on top of the spread. Cover the top of the banana with more spread. Fold edges of pastry over banana and roll up to enclose. Place on a lightly greased baking tray. Brush lightly with beaten egg. Bake at 220°C for 12 minutes or until golden. Serve warm, dusted with icing sugar. **Makes 8 parcels**.

Cook's Hint: *Kids will love these little treats!*

mushroom and bacon frittata

1 tablespoon Rizzoli pure olive oil
4 rashers rindless bacon, chopped
200 g button mushrooms, sliced
1 teaspoon crushed garlic
½ cup cream
8 eggs, lightly beaten
½ cup freshly grated parmesan cheese
1 tablespoon wholegrain mustard
salt and freshly ground black pepper to season
Quality Bakers Turkish bread, toasted, to serve (see page 12)

Heat oil in a heavy-based frying pan. Cook bacon, mushrooms and garlic for 6–8 minutes until pan is dry. Combine bacon mixture, cream, eggs, parmesan, mustard and salt and pepper in a bowl. Grease a 23-cm-round cake tin. Line base with baking paper. Pour in frittata mixture. Bake at 180°C for 30–35 minutes or until egg mixture is set and golden. Stand for 10 minutes before turning out. Cut into wedges and serve warm accompanied by toasted Turkish bread. **Serves 4**.

eggs benedict

Hollandaise Sauce
50 g butter
1 tablespoon lemon juice
2 egg yolks
¼ cup cream
½ teaspoon dry mustard
¼ teaspoon salt

8 rashers rindless bacon*
8 eggs
4 Quality Bakers English Muffin Splits
freshly ground black pepper to garnish

To make the hollandaise, melt butter in a double boiler. Add lemon juice, egg yolks and cream. Cook, stirring constantly, until thick and smooth. Do not boil or sauce will curdle. Remove from heat. Add mustard and salt and beat until smooth. Grill bacon until beginning to crisp. Split muffins in half and toast. Meanwhile, pour 4–5 cm of water into a deep frying pan. Bring to the boil, then reduce heat to a simmer. Break eggs into the pan. Cook for 3 minutes or until cooked to your liking. Place 2 muffins on each serving plate. Top each muffin with a rasher of bacon and an egg. Drizzle with hollandaise. Garnish with a sprinkling of pepper. Serve immediately. **Serves 4**.

*Sliced ham can be substituted for the bacon. It does not require grilling.

Cook's Hint: *For smaller appetites, serve a half portion.*

scrambled eggs
on toast

6 eggs
⅓ cup milk
salt and freshly ground black pepper
1 tablespoon butter
2 tablespoons chopped parsley
Quality Bakers Nature's Fresh toast-cut bread, toasted
sprig of Italian parsley to garnish

Lightly beat eggs. Stir in milk. Season to taste with salt and pepper. Melt butter in a heavy-based saucepan. Pour in eggs. Cook over a low heat for about 5 minutes, stirring constantly with a wooden spoon. As the eggs cook on the base of the pan, fold them back into the uncooked egg on top. When the eggs are creamy and thick, remove from heat and stir in parsley. Toast bread, place on serving plates and pile scrambled eggs on top. Garnish with a sprig of parsley. **Serves 4**.

Cook's Hint: *For creamy scrambled eggs, use cream instead of the milk.*

slow-roasted tomatoes
and grilled mushrooms
with toasted turkish bread

8 tomatoes (preferably Roma tomatoes), halved
Rizzoli extra virgin olive oil to drizzle
Rizzoli balsamic vinegar to drizzle
salt and freshly ground black pepper to season
8 portobello mushrooms
Quality Bakers Turkish bread, toasted, to serve (see page 12)
sprigs of basil to garnish (optional)

Place tomatoes cut-side up in a roasting dish. Drizzle over a little oil, then vinegar. Sprinkle with salt and pepper. Bake at 150ºC for 1 hour or until tender. Remove from oven. Place mushrooms on a baking tray, stem-side up. Drizzle with olive oil. Grill for 2–3 minutes until tender. To serve, arrange 4 tomato halves, 2 mushrooms and toasted bread on 4 serving plates. Garnish with sprigs of basil. **Serves 4**.

freshly
baked

Any of these wonderful recipes can be

made the night before needed and make a

great addition to the lunchbox for all

members of the household. What about

Date and Orange Scones or Spinach, Red

Capsicum and Cheese Muffins for morning

tea? Or Gingerbread Loaf for afternoon tea

or to take on a weekend picnic lunch to

the beach or park? Your family and friends

will reward you with compliments galore

— try some and see!

sundried tomato
and basil muffins

3 cups Champion standard grade flour
4 teaspoons Edmonds baking powder
1 teaspoon salt
¼ teaspoon freshly ground black pepper
1 cup grated tasty cheddar cheese
⅓ cup drained sundried tomatoes, chopped
2 tablespoons chopped basil
1½ cups milk
⅓ cup Amco canola oil
2 eggs
1 tablespoon tomato paste
2 tablespoons pinenuts (optional)

Preheat oven to 200°C. Grease 12 deep muffin tins. Combine flour, baking powder, salt and pepper in a large bowl. Stir in cheese, sundried tomatoes and basil. In another bowl, whisk together milk, oil, eggs and tomato paste. Pour liquid ingredients over dry ingredients. Mix lightly until ingredients are just combined. Do not overmix. Divide mixture between prepared tins. Sprinkle pinenuts over top of muffins. Bake for 20–25 minutes until golden. Stand muffins for 5 minutes before removing from tins. **Makes 12 large muffins**.

spinach, red capsicum and cheese muffins

1 red capsicum
2 cups shredded spinach leaves
2½ cups Champion standard grade flour
4 teaspoons Edmonds baking powder
1 teaspoon salt
¼ teaspoon freshly ground black pepper
¼ teaspoon ground nutmeg
1 cup grated tasty cheddar cheese
⅓ cup freshly grated parmesan cheese
1½ cups milk
⅓ cup Amco canola oil
2 eggs

Preheat oven grill. Place capsicum on a baking tray. Grill about 10 cm from heat source, turning frequently, until skin blisters and begins to blacken. Transfer to a small heatproof bowl. Cover bowl and allow capsicum to cool. Peel off skin, cut in half and remove seeds. Thinly slice the flesh. Place spinach in a microwave-proof container with 2 tablespoons water. Cook on high power for 30 seconds. Stand for 1 minute, then drain thoroughly and squeeze out excess liquid. Preheat oven to 200°C. Grease 12 deep muffin tins. Combine flour, baking powder, salt, pepper and nutmeg in a large bowl. Stir in sliced capsicum, spinach and cheeses. In another bowl, whisk together milk, oil and eggs. Pour liquid ingredients over dry ingredients. Mix lightly until ingredients are just combined. Do not overmix. Divide mixture between prepared tins. Bake for 20–25 minutes until golden. Stand muffins for 5 minutes before removing from tins. **Makes 12 large muffins**.

Cook's Hint: *Baby spinach leaves produced for salads are ideal for use in these muffins.*

lemon sour cream muffins

3 cups Champion standard grade flour
1 cup sugar
4 teaspoons Edmonds baking powder
2 tablespoons finely grated lemon zest
125 g butter, melted and cooled slightly
1¼ cups milk
125 g (½ cup) sour cream
2 eggs
2 tablespoons lemon juice

Lemon Syrup
¼ cup sugar
¼ cup lemon juice

Preheat oven to 200°C. Grease 12 deep muffin tins. Combine flour, sugar, baking powder and zest in a large mixing bowl. In another bowl, whisk together butter, milk, sour cream, eggs and lemon juice. Pour milk mixture over dry ingredients. Mix lightly until just combined. Do not overmix. Divide mixture between prepared tins. Bake for 20-25 minutes or until risen and light golden. While muffins are cooking, prepare the lemon syrup. Combine sugar and lemon juice in a small saucepan. Stir over a low heat until sugar dissolves. Bring to the boil, reduce heat and simmer for 3–4 minutes. When muffins are cooked, use a metal skewer to pierce 4–5 holes in each muffin. Brush syrup over hot muffins. Stand for 5 minutes before removing from tins. **Makes 12 large muffins**.

Variation: *Lemon Sour Cream Popovers* — cook the above mixture in 12 greased popover tins for 20 minutes. When cooked, transfer to a wire rack to cool. To serve, wrap a strip of baking paper around each popover and tie with curling ribbon or string. Insert a lemon leaf between the ribbon and paper.

date and orange scones

3 cups Champion standard grade flour
6 teaspoons Edmonds baking powder
½ teaspoon cinnamon
¼ teaspoon salt
75 g butter, chopped
1 cup chopped pitted dates
1 tablespoon finely grated orange zest
1–1½ cups milk
extra milk to brush

Preheat oven to 220°C. Lightly dust a baking tray with flour. Sift flour, baking powder, cinnamon and salt into a large bowl. Cut butter into flour until it resembles fine breadcrumbs. (This can be done in a food processor.) Stir in dates and zest. Add sufficient milk to mix quickly to a soft dough, using a knife. Knead lightly, then transfer dough to the baking tray. Press into a rectangle about 3 cm thick. Cut into 9 equal-sized pieces. Leave a 2-cm space between scones. Brush tops with milk. Bake for 10 minutes until golden. **Makes 9 scones**.

blueberry cream cheese loaf

125 g butter, softened
100 g cream cheese, softened
1¼ cups sugar
3 eggs
1 teaspoon vanilla essence
2 teaspoons finely grated lemon zest
1½ cups Champion standard grade flour
1½ teaspoons Edmonds baking powder
1 cup blueberries (fresh or frozen*)

Beat butter, cream cheese and sugar until light and creamy. Add eggs one at a time, beating well after each addition. Beat in essence and zest. Sift flour and baking powder. Fold into creamed mixture. Lightly fold in blueberries. Grease a 20-cm x 11-cm (base measurement) loaf tin. Line the base with baking paper. Transfer mixture to prepared tin. Bake at 180°C for about 1 hour or until a skewer inserted in the centre of the loaf comes out clean. Stand for 5 minutes before transferring to a wire rack to cool. Slice and serve with butter.

*If using frozen blueberries, do not allow them to thaw before use.

gingerbread loaf

125 g butter, softened
½ cup sugar
½ cup golden syrup
1 egg
2½ cups Champion standard grade flour
2 teaspoons Edmonds baking powder
1½ teaspoons Edmonds baking soda
1½ teaspoons ground ginger
½ teaspoon cinnamon
¾ cup warm water

Preheat oven to 180°C. Grease a 20-cm x 11-cm loaf tin (base measurement). Line the base with baking paper. Beat butter and sugar together until light and creamy. Warm golden syrup slightly and add to creamed mixture. Beat well. Beat in egg. Sift flour, baking powder, baking soda and spices. Fold into creamed mixture alternately with water. Transfer mixture to prepared tin. Bake for 45 minutes until well risen. Stand for 5 minutes before transferring to a wire rack. Serve warm or at room temperature, accompanied by butter to spread.

almond and chocolate friands

1½ cups icing sugar
½ cup Champion standard grade flour
100 g ground almonds
50 g dark chocolate, grated
5 egg whites, lightly beaten
175 g butter, melted and cooled slightly
icing sugar to dust

Preheat oven to 200°C. Grease 9 x ½-cup-capacity friand moulds (or muffin tins). Dust lightly with flour. Sift icing sugar and flour into a bowl. Stir in almonds and chocolate. Add egg whites and stir until ingredients are just combined. Add butter and mix until smooth. Divide mixture between prepared tins. Bake for 20 minutes or until a skewer inserted in the centre comes out clean. Stand friands for 5 minutes before removing from tins. Cool on a wire rack. Before serving, dust lightly with icing sugar. **Makes 9 friands**.

apple and walnut filo parcels

380 g can diced apple
½ cup chopped walnuts
¼ cup currants
⅓ cup sugar
finely grated zest of 1 lemon
1 teaspoon ground cinnamon
12 sheets Irvines filo pastry
3 tablespoons melted butter
icing sugar to dust
crème fraîche or whipped cream to serve

Preheat oven to 190°C. Combine apple, walnuts, currants, sugar, zest and cinnamon in a bowl. To make each parcel, lay a sheet of filo on a flat surface. Brush lightly with butter. Fold in half by taking one of the short edges over to meet the other short edge. Brush lightly with butter, then fold in half again by taking one of the short edges across to meet the other short edge. Place 3 tablespoons of apple mixture on the centre of the pastry. Gather pastry up around mixture, forming a purse and pinching to enclose. Repeat until all parcels are made. Place on a lightly greased baking tray. Brush with butter. Bake for 12 minutes until golden. Dust with icing sugar and serve with crème fraîche or whipped cream. **Makes 12**.

brioche

1 tablespoon sugar
½ cup warm milk
3 teaspoons Edmonds active yeast
3 cups Champion high grade flour
1½ teaspoons salt
4 eggs
175 g butter, cut into cubes and softened

Glaze
1 egg
1 tablespoon water

Dissolve sugar in the warm milk. Sprinkle yeast over milk, then stir until dissolved. Set aside in a warm place for 10 minutes until frothy. Place 1 cup of the flour and the salt in the bowl of a food processor fitted with a metal blade. Add frothy yeast mixture and pulse until combined. Add eggs, one at a time, pulsing for about 30 seconds between each addition. Gradually add a further 1 cup of the flour. Process for 30 seconds. Add butter and process for a further 30 seconds. Finally, add remaining 1 cup of flour and process for 2 minutes until dough is smooth and creamy. The dough should be very soft and almost batter-like. Place dough in a greased bowl. Cover and stand in a warm place until doubled in bulk (about 1 hour). Gently punch down the dough. Cover with plastic wrap and refrigerate for 12 hours or overnight. Transfer dough to a lightly floured surface. Divide dough into equal portions that will half fill brioche moulds or muffin tins of your choice. To shape each brioche, take a portion of dough and break off one-eighth. Roll both pieces into balls. Place large ball in greased brioche mould or muffin tin. Using scissors, snip a cross in the top of the large ball. Push a finger halfway down into the dough. Sit the small ball in the indentation. Cover brioche with plastic wrap and stand in a warm place until doubled in size (about 1 hour). To make glaze, whisk together egg and water. Brush brioches lightly with glaze. Bake at 200°C for 12–15 minutes until golden. Remove from moulds and cool on a wire rack.

Cook's Hint: *Brioche are delicious served with Lemon Curd (see page 20).*

soups

These tasty and nourishing soups are easy to

prepare and just the thing for a winter lunch or

dinner, but can of course be enjoyed at any

time of the year. They can be made in advance

and reheated in a saucepan or in the

microwave. Served with the suggested Soup

Accompaniments or with fresh crusty bread,

they are filling, hearty and delicious.

spicy pumpkin soup

750 g pumpkin, peeled and seeded
2 large potatoes, peeled and quartered
2 tablespoons Amco canola oil
2 onions, finely chopped
1 teaspoon crushed garlic
1 tablespoon grated root ginger
½ teaspoon garam masala
1 tablespoon Champion standard grade flour
650 ml chicken stock
¼ cup chopped fresh herbs, e.g. parsley, thyme, rosemary
salt and freshly ground black pepper to season
chives to garnish
Blue Cheese Bruschetta (see page 42) to serve

Cut pumpkin into chunks. Cook pumpkin and potatoes in boiling water, or microwave, until tender. Drain and mash. Heat oil in a saucepan. Cook onion for 5 minutes until soft. Add garlic, ginger and garam masala and cook for 2 minutes, stirring constantly. Add flour and cook for a further 2 minutes, stirring constantly. Remove from heat. Gradually add stock, stirring to blend. Return to a low heat and stir until sauce boils. Stir in mashed vegetables. Bring to the boil. Simmer for 5 minutes. Stir in herbs and season to taste. Ladle hot soup into warm bowls. **Serves 4**.

buttermilk hot cakes with banana, strawberries, crème fraîche and maple syrup (top) 17
corn fritters with crispy bacon and turkish bread (bottom) 47

minestrone

1 tablespoon Rizzoli pure olive oil
1 onion, chopped
2 cloves garlic, crushed
2 rashers rindless bacon, chopped
1 stalk celery, sliced
1 medium potato, peeled and diced
2 carrots, peeled and diced
2 x 400 g cans tomatoes in juice, chopped
1 tablespoon tomato paste
3 cups chicken or vegetable stock
½ cup Diamond macaroni
300 g can butter beans, drained and rinsed
½ cup sliced green beans
½ cup frozen peas
salt and freshly ground black pepper to season
Parmesan Wafers (see page 42) to serve

Heat oil in a large saucepan. Cook onion, garlic and bacon for 5 minutes until onion is soft. Add celery, potato, carrot, tomatoes, tomato paste, stock and macaroni. Bring to the boil. Reduce heat and simmer for 30 minutes. Add beans and peas and simmer for a further 10 minutes. Season to taste. Ladle hot soup into warm bowls. Accompany with Parmesan Wafers. **Serves 4–6**.

minestrone (top right) 39
soup accompaniments — pizza bread soup dippers, blue cheese bruschetta,
parmesan wafers (top left) 42
spicy pumpkin soup (bottom) 38

thai-style chicken soup

300 g boneless chicken breasts or thighs
1 tablespoon Amco canola oil
1 onion, finely chopped
1 teaspoon crushed garlic
2 teaspoons ground cumin
½ teaspoon turmeric
¼ teaspoon chilli powder
finely grated zest and juice of 2 limes
1 litre chicken stock
400 ml can coconut cream
2 tablespoons fish sauce
2 tablespoons chopped coriander
salt and freshly ground black pepper to season

Remove skin and fat from chicken and discard. Cut chicken into thin slices, about 3–4 cm in length. Heat oil in a large saucepan. Cook onion, garlic and spices for 5 minutes until onion is soft. Add lime zest and juice, chicken stock, coconut cream and fish sauce. Bring to the boil over a medium heat. Add chicken and simmer gently for 10 minutes until chicken is cooked. Stir in coriander and season to taste. Ladle into warm bowls. **Serves 4**.

creamy tomato
and basil soup

1 tablespoon Rizzoli pure olive oil
1 onion, finely chopped
1 teaspoon crushed garlic
2 x 400 g cans tomatoes in juice, chopped
1 tablespoon sugar
375 ml chicken or vegetable stock
½ cup light cream
2 tablespoons shredded basil leaves
salt and freshly ground black pepper to season
shredded basil leaves to garnish
Garlic Parmesan Croutons (see page 42) to serve

Heat oil in a large, heavy-based saucepan. Cook onion for 4–5 minutes until soft. Add garlic, tomatoes, sugar and stock. Bring to the boil. Reduce heat and simmer for 20 minutes. Purée in batches in a food processor. Return to saucepan. Add cream and basil. Heat gently — do not allow to boil. Season to taste. Ladle into warm bowls. Garnish with basil. Serve with Garlic Parmesan Croutons. **Serves 4**.

soup accompaniments

garlic parmesan croutons

¼ cup Rizzoli pure olive oil
1 clove garlic, crushed
½ loaf French bread, cut on the diagonal into 1.5-cm thick slices
2 tablespoons freshly grated parmesan cheese

Combine oil and garlic. Brush bread slices all over with oil mixture. Place on a baking tray. Sprinkle over parmesan. Bake at 190°C for 15 minutes, turning once.

parmesan wafers

¾ cup finely grated parmesan cheese*

Place heaped teaspoonfuls of the grated cheese on a greased baking tray, forming a 4-cm-diameter circle with the cheese and allowing room for spreading. Bake at 190°C for 5 minutes until the cheese has melted and formed a wafer. Leave wafers on tray for 30 seconds, then, working quickly, use a spatula to transfer them to a wire rack. **Makes 24 wafers**.

*Use freshly grated (not pre-grated) parmesan cheese for these wafers.

blue cheese bruschetta

1 loaf French bread
Rizzoli pure olive oil to brush
200 g blue cheese, crumbled

Cut French bread into 1-cm-thick diagonal slices. Brush both sides of bread with oil. Place in a single layer on a baking tray. Bake at 190°C for 6–8 minutes until light golden. Remove from oven and scatter crumbled cheese over bruschetta. Return to oven until cheese begins to melt and bubble. **Serve warm**.

pizza bread soup dippers

Rizzoli extra virgin olive oil to brush
crushed garlic
Leaning Tower pizza bases
freshly grated parmesan cheese, rosemary leaves or rock salt
  to sprinkle

Preheat oven to 200°C. Place an oven tray in oven to heat. Combine oil with crushed garlic. Brush pizza bases generously with oil mixture. Sprinkle with parmesan, rosemary or rock salt. Transfer pizza to hot oven tray. Bake for 10–12 minutes until golden. Use a pizza wheel to cut into wedges. Dip hot pizza wedges into hot soup.

lunch and light bites

Spoil your friends — make two or three

of these interesting recipes and serve for

a relaxed weekend brunch with a glass of

chilled white wine or freshly squeezed

fruit juice. Alternatively, try the Panini,

Muffins or Melts after a hectic morning's

schedule and be surprised at how quick

they are to assemble, and how more-ish.

Great as a quick snack before the movies

— and your kids will love them too.

muffin splits

Quality Bakers Muffin Splits provide the perfect base for delicious breakfast or brunch meals. With five flavours of muffins to choose from, the topping combinations are endless! Try one of our favourites:

english muffins

Split muffin in half and toast. Top with poached or scrambled eggs and garnish with a slice of grilled bacon or smoked salmon.

spicy fruit muffins

Split muffin in half and toast. Spread with butter and top with sliced banana. Squeeze lemon juice over the banana, then sprinkle with brown sugar. Place under a preheated grill until the sugar melts.

cheese muffins

Split muffin in half and toast. Spread sparingly with wholegrain mustard and top with panfried mushrooms. Garnish with strips of red capsicum.

cheese and bacon muffins

Split muffin in half and toast. Spread with butter and top with a poached egg. Garnish with finely chopped parsley.

apricot muffins

Split muffin and toast. Spread with cream cheese and top with drained, canned apricot halves. Sprinkle brown sugar over apricots and place under a preheated grill to caramelise (until brown sugar is melted and bubbly).

blueberry cream cheese loaf (top) 32
lemon sour cream muffins (middle) 30
almond and chocolate friands (bottom) 34

melts

A melt is a delicious, satisfying snack or light meal that can be made using a wide variety of breads and endless combinations of topping ingredients. Always include cheese, which melts when placed under a grill (hence the name 'melt'). Mozzarella cheese is a good choice, as it has great melting properties, but a cheddar-style cheese is also good. Quality Bakers Turkish bread is ideal for melts:

- Cut desired lengths of bread from the loaf, then cut in half horizontally.
- Brush cut surfaces lightly with Rizzoli extra virgin olive oil, then toast lightly under a preheated grill.
- Layer with ingredients of your choice, finishing with sliced cheese.
- Place on a baking tray, then grill until the cheese melts and begins to bubble.

Topping Suggestions
- Flaked, drained canned tuna, sliced tomatoes and thinly sliced red onion.
- Grilled rindless bacon rashers and sliced avocado.
- Roasted red capsicum, halved pitted olives, thinly sliced red onion, toasted pinenuts and shredded basil leaves.
- Pickle, cooked shredded chicken and blanched asparagus.
- Sliced ham, sliced tomato and sliced avocado.

english muffin splits with scrambled eggs and smoked salmon (top left) 44
melts with tuna, tomato and red onion (top right) 45
panini with bacon, avocado, tomato and cheese (bottom) 46

panini

Quality Bakers panini are a range of flatbreads that can be assembled with any combination of fillings and are best served warm after being cooked in a panini maker or toasted-sandwich maker. Panini can also be cooked under a grill or in a lightly greased frying pan.

Use a bread knife to slice open the panini lengthwise, then fill as desired. Cook filled panini in a toasted-sandwich maker or lightly greased frying pan for 3–5 minutes.

Filling Suggestions
- Chicken, Pesto and Roasted Red Capsicum — spread cut surfaces of the panini with pesto. Fill with shredded cooked chicken and strips of roasted red capsicum.
- Ham, Mozzarella and Tomato — fill with sliced ham, sliced tomato and sliced mozzarella cheese.
- Bacon, Avocado, Tomato and Cheese — grill rashers of rindless bacon until crisp. Allow 2 rashers of bacon per panini and top with sliced avocado, sliced tomato and sliced mozzarella or tasty cheddar cheese.
- Grilled Vegetable and Feta — if desired, spread cut surfaces of panini with pesto. Top with sliced feta cheese and grilled vegetables — capsicums, courgettes and asparagus (see page 11 for instructions on grilling vegetables).
- Smoked Salmon, Avocado and Cream Cheese — spread the lower half of the panini with a generous amount of cream cheese. Arrange smoked salmon and sliced avocado on top.

Cook's Hint: *Italian for 'little breads', panini are the perfect base for a delicious snack or light meal.*

corn fritters
with crispy bacon
and turkish bread

1 cup Champion standard grade flour
1 teaspoon Edmonds baking powder
½ teaspoon Edmonds baking soda
¼ teaspoon salt
freshly ground black pepper to season
2 eggs, lightly beaten
²/₃ cup milk
2 tablespoons melted butter
1 cup drained canned kernel corn
1 spring onion, finely chopped
1 tablespoon chopped parsley
8 rashers rindless bacon
butter to grease
Italian parsley to garnish
Quality Bakers Turkish bread, toasted, to serve (see page 12)
sweet chilli sauce to serve

Sift flour, baking powder, baking soda, salt and pepper into a bowl. Add eggs, milk and melted butter and mix lightly to combine. Fold in corn, spring onion and parsley. Heat a heavy-based frying pan greased with a little butter. Drop tablespoons of mixture into pan. Cook for about 2 minutes or until bubbles appear on the surface. Turn and cook other side. Remove from pan and keep warm while cooking remaining fritters. Grill bacon until beginning to crisp. To serve, layer 3 fritters with 2 rashers of bacon. Garnish with a sprig of parsley. Accompany with toasted Turkish bread and sweet chilli sauce. **Serves 4**.

Cook's Hint: *The fritter batter can be prepared up to 2 hours ahead of time. Cover and refrigerate until required.*

spinach frittata

2 tablespoons Rizzoli pure olive oil
1 onion, finely diced
100 g baby spinach leaves*, roughly chopped
9 eggs
¼ teaspoon ground nutmeg
salt and freshly ground black pepper to season
1 cup grated tasty cheddar cheese
¼ cup freshly grated parmesan cheese

Heat oil in a 25-cm-diameter heavy-based frying pan with a heatproof handle. Cook onion for 4–5 minutes until soft. Stir in spinach. Cook for 2–3 minutes until wilted. Spread onion and spinach mixture evenly over base of pan. Reduce heat to very low. Preheat oven grill. Beat together eggs, nutmeg and salt and pepper. Pour into pan. Allow the eggs to set for 10 seconds then, with a heatproof rubber spatula, and starting at the centre, gently stir the eggs. Lift up the edges of the setting frittata so egg flows to the base. When the frittata is half set, sprinkle over both cheeses. Place pan under grill for 3–4 minutes until frittata is golden and set. Remove from oven and stand for 3–4 minutes before cutting into wedges. **Serves 4**.

*Baby spinach leaves sold for spinach salad are ideal for this recipe.

Cook's Hint: *Frittata is also delicious served at room temperature. Try slicing thinly and using as a sandwich filling.*

spinach and cheese soufflé

melted butter to grease dishes
2 cups shredded spinach, washed
2 tablespoons water
3 tablespoons butter
3 tablespoons Champion standard grade flour
1 cup milk
1 cup grated tasty cheddar cheese
1 teaspoon cayenne pepper
pinch of nutmeg
salt and freshly ground black pepper
4 eggs, separated

Thoroughly brush a 15-cm-diameter soufflé dish or four 10-cm-diameter soufflé dishes with melted butter. Place spinach and water in a saucepan. Cover and cook over a medium heat just until spinach wilts — about 2 minutes. Drain in a sieve. Refresh under cold running water. Squeeze out excess liquid. Melt butter in a medium saucepan. Add flour and stir for 2 minutes. Remove from heat. Gradually add milk, stirring constantly. Return pan to heat, stirring continuously until sauce thickens and comes to the boil. Remove from heat. Stir in cheese, cayenne pepper and nutmeg. Season. Cool slightly. Stir in spinach. Add egg yolks one at a time, beating well. Using an electric mixer, beat egg whites to a stiff foam. Carefully fold half the egg whites into the sauce. Carefully fold sauce mixture into remaining egg whites. Spoon mixture into prepared dish to three-quarters full. Place into a heatproof dish. Pour hot water into the outer dish to come within 3 cm of the top of the soufflé. Bake at 180°C for 40–45 minutes or until risen and golden. For individual soufflés, bake for 30–35 minutes. **Serves 3–4 as a light meal**.

rustic caramelised onion and tomato tarts

3 tablespoons Rizzoli pure olive oil
4 red onions, thinly sliced
2 tablespoons brown sugar
2 tablespoons Rizzoli balsamic vinegar
400 g Irvines flaky puff pastry
24 cherry tomatoes, halved
salt and freshly ground black pepper to season
⅓ cup finely grated parmesan cheese to sprinkle

Heat oil in a heavy-based frying pan. Cook onions over a very low heat for 20 minutes, stirring regularly. Stir in brown sugar and vinegar and cook for a further 2 minutes. Cool. Roll pastry out into a 32-cm x 24-cm rectangle. Cut into 4 equal-sized rectangles. Line a baking tray with baking paper. Transfer pastry rectangles to the tray. Refrigerate for 15 minutes. Divide caramelised onion between the pastry, spreading evenly and leaving a 3-cm border. Arrange tomatoes cut-side up on top of onion. Season and sprinkle with parmesan. Bake at 200ºC for 20 minutes or until the pastry border is risen and golden. Accompany with a tossed salad. **Serves 4**.

rustic caramelised onion and tomato tarts (top) 50
broccoli and blue cheese filo pie (bottom) 51

broccoli and blue cheese filo pie

1 small head broccoli, cut into florets
3 tablespoons melted butter
6 sheets Irvines filo pastry, thawed
100 g blue cheese, crumbled
5 eggs, lightly beaten
1½ cups milk
½ cup cream
salt and freshly ground black pepper to season
¼ cup finely grated parmesan cheese

Place broccoli in a microwave-proof dish. Add 1 tablespoon of water. Cover and cook on high power for 45 seconds. Tip into a sieve and refresh under cold running water. Drain thoroughly. Brush a 25-cm x 20-cm baking dish with melted butter. Line with a sheet of filo, extending the pastry over the ends of the dish. Brush with melted butter. Repeat the last two steps, layering the sheets of pastry and brushing with butter. Scatter broccoli and cheese over base of dish. Whisk together eggs, milk, cream and salt and pepper. Pour into dish. Sprinkle over parmesan. Scrunch up the overhanging pastry and place on the edge of the pie. Bake at 190°C for 30–35 minutes or until egg mixture is set. Stand for 4–5 minutes before serving. Serve with a tossed salad. **Serves 4**.

vegetable, cashew nut and hokkien noodle stir-fry (right) 69
pumpkin and feta lasagne (left) 71

pumpkin and chicken filo pies

2 cups (275 g) peeled, seeded and diced pumpkin
1 large potato, peeled and diced
1 tablespoon butter to mash
2 tablespoons Amco canola oil
2 onions, finely chopped
2 teaspoons ground cumin
1 teaspoon garam masala
1 single boneless, skinless chicken breast, diced
1 teaspoon crushed garlic
1 cup grated tasty cheddar cheese
salt and freshly ground black pepper to season
50 g butter, melted
18 sheets Irvines filo pastry

Cook the pumpkin and potato until tender. Drain. Add the butter and mash. Heat the oil in a frying pan and cook onion, cumin, garam masala and chicken for 6–8 minutes until onion is soft. Add the garlic and cook for 2 minutes. Combine mashed vegetable mixture, chicken mixture and cheese. Season. Brush 12 deep muffin tins with melted butter. For each pie, lightly brush a sheet of filo pastry with melted butter. Fold in half widthways, then brush with butter. Fold in half again. Line prepared tins with the pastry. Spoon the filling into pastry shells. Cut the remaining 6 sheets of filo pastry in half widthways. Scrunch each portion into a ball and place on top of pies. Brush with melted butter. Bake at 190°C for 20 minutes until golden. Stand for 8–10 minutes before serving. **Makes 12 pies**.

hearty salads

Feel like something light but substantial? These

salads are excellent to accompany a barbecue, to

eat as a main course and especially to share with

friends. When you need something a little more

than a snack, any of these salads will fit the bill

and titillate the tastebuds. The Pasta and

Roasted Winter Vegetable Salad is an excellent

choice for vegetarians.

warm potato
and bacon salad

6 medium potatoes
a little Rizzoli pure olive oil to cook
6 rashers rindless bacon, diced
4 spring onions, chopped
½ cup toasted pinenuts (see page 12)
¼ cup chopped sundried tomatoes

Dressing
¾ cup mayonnaise
¾ cup sour cream (light or regular)
2 tablespoons basil pesto
salt and freshly ground black pepper to season

Scrub potatoes and cut into 2-cm cubes. Microwave or boil potato cubes until tender. Drain thoroughly. While the potatoes are cooking, heat a little oil in a heavy-based frying pan. Cook bacon over a medium heat for 6–8 minutes, stirring occasionally until it begins to crisp. Combine all salad ingredients in a bowl. To make the dressing, combine all ingredients. Pour dressing over salad and toss gently to coat. Serve immediately. **Serves 4 as a light meal**.

Cook's Hint: *Choose waxy potatoes for salad making — they hold their shape once cooked and do not fall apart. Waxy varieties include Nadine, Draga, Jersey Benne and Frisia.*

tandoori chicken salad

4 single boneless, skinless chicken breasts
¼ cup Patak's tandoori curry paste
2 tablespoons natural unsweetened yoghurt
4 handfuls mixed salad greens
1 tablespoon Rizzoli extra virgin olive oil
1 tablespoon DYC white wine vinegar
2 bananas
1 tablespoon lemon juice
¼ cup coconut, toasted (see page 12)
4 naan breads*
1 avocado, sliced
Patak's mango chutney to serve

Place chicken between 2 sheets of plastic wrap. Pound with a heavy object (such as a rolling pin) to flatten to an even thickness of 1 cm. Place in a single layer in a plastic or glass dish. Combine curry paste and yoghurt and spread over chicken. Cover and refrigerate for 1 hour. Preheat oven grill. Grill chicken for 6–8 minutes on each side or until cooked through. Cool. Place salad greens in a bowl. Sprinkle over oil and vinegar and toss to coat. Peel and slice bananas. Place in a small bowl. Add lemon juice and toss to coat, then sprinkle over coconut, tossing to coat. To assemble salad, place a naan bread on individual serving plates. Top with salad greens. Slice chicken and arrange with avocado on top of salad greens. Place a spoonful of banana slices on the side and serve with a dollop of mango chutney. **Serves 4 as a light meal**.

*Naan, an Indian bread, is available from Indian restaurants or from some supermarket freezers. Naan bread mixes are also available.

broad bean, mushroom and spicy sausage salad

200 g frozen broad beans
200 g button mushrooms, washed
150 g chorizo sausage*, sliced
2 tablespoons chopped chives

Dressing
2 tablespoons Rizzoli extra virgin olive oil
2 tablespoons freshly squeezed orange juice
2 teaspoons grainy mustard
½ teaspoon finely grated orange zest

Cook beans in boiling water for 3–4 minutes until just tender. Tip into a sieve and rinse under cold running water, then plunge into a bowl of iced water to refresh. To peel beans, pierce the skin on the rounded side of the bean, gently squeeze the opposite side and the bean will pop out. Discard skins. Combine all salad ingredients in a bowl. To make the dressing, combine all ingredients Pour dressing over salad. Toss to coat. **Serves 4 as a light meal**.

*Chorizo sausage is a spicy Spanish sausage available from most supermarket delis.

Cook's Hint: *The slightly time-consuming procedure of peeling each bean is well rewarded with a very tasty, satisfying salad.*

pasta and roasted winter vegetable salad

1 medium golden kumara (about 275 g), peeled
500 g pumpkin, seeded and peeled
2 carrots, peeled
1 red onion, peeled
¼ cup **Rizzoli** extra virgin olive oil
1 teaspoon crushed garlic
2 tablespoons rosemary leaves
rock (or ordinary) salt to sprinkle
250 g **Diamond** pasta shapes, e.g. torroncini or ricciolini
¼ cup basil pesto
⅓ cup toasted pumpkin seeds (see page 12)

Preheat oven to 220ºC. Cut kumara and pumpkin into bite-size chunks. Cut carrots on the diagonal into 5-mm-thick slices. Cut onion into quarters, then cut each piece in half. Pour oil over the base of a roasting dish. Place in oven for 2–3 minutes to heat. Remove pan from oven and add vegetables, garlic and rosemary. Sprinkle over salt and toss to coat. Cook for 15–20 minutes, turning occasionally until vegetables are tender (but not mushy) and golden. Allow to cool to room temperature. Cook pasta according to instructions on packet. Tip into a sieve. Refresh under cold running water and drain thoroughly. Combine pasta, pesto, vegetables and pumpkin seeds in a bowl. Toss gently. **Serves 4–5 as a light meal**.

Cook's Hint: *For a warm salad, toss hot vegetables through the drained, cooled pasta and serve immediately.*

warm ginger chicken, crispy noodle and cashew nut salad

4 single boneless, skinless chicken breasts
¼ cup soy sauce
2 tablespoons lemon juice
1 tablespoon Amco peanut oil
1 tablespoon finely grated root ginger
2 carrots, peeled
10-cm length telegraph cucumber
2 cups mung beans
2 cups crispy noodles
½ cup roasted salted cashew nuts

Dressing
2 tablespoons soy sauce
1 tablespoon sesame oil
1 tablespoon lemon juice
1 tablespoon chopped coriander
coriander leaves to garnish

Place chicken between 2 sheets of plastic wrap. Pound with a heavy object (such as a rolling pin) to flatten to an even thickness of 1 cm. Place in a single layer in a plastic or glass dish. Combine first measures of soy sauce, lemon juice, peanut oil and ginger. Pour over chicken, turning to coat. Cover and refrigerate for at least 1 hour. Using a vegetable peeler, peel strips from the carrots. Plunge into boiling water for 30 seconds. Tip into a sieve and refresh under cold running water. Drain. Cut cucumber into diagonal slices, then cut slices in half lengthwise. Grill or barbecue chicken for 6–8 minutes on each side or until cooked through. Stand for 3–4 minutes before slicing. Combine chicken, carrot ribbons, cucumber, mung beans, noodles and nuts in a bowl. To make the dressing, combine all ingredients. Pour dressing over salad and toss to combine. Pile salad onto 4 serving plates. Garnish with coriander leaves and serve immediately. **Serves 4 as a light meal.**

main
meals

Substantial, filling, mouth-watering

choices in this Main Meals selection

provide something for everyone. What

better than sitting by an open fire away

from the evening chill eating succulent

Osso Buco or Hearty Beef Goulash.

Leftovers are equally as good reheated for

lunch the following day.

blue cheese and walnut stuffed chicken breasts

1 cup fresh white breadcrumbs (see page 11)
100 g blue cheese, crumbled
½ cup chopped walnuts
2 spring onions, sliced
2 tablespoons chopped coriander
1 egg
salt and freshly ground black pepper to season
4 single boneless, skinless chicken breasts
12 rashers streaky rindless bacon
liquid honey to drizzle

To make the stuffing, combine breadcrumbs, cheese, walnuts, spring onions, coriander, egg and salt and pepper in a bowl. Mix well. Trim visible fat from chicken. Place chicken between 2 sheets of plastic wrap. Pound with a heavy object (such as a rolling pin) to flatten to an even thickness of 6 mm. Cover half of each breast with stuffing, then fold over to enclose. Wrap 3 rashers of bacon around each parcel to cover. Place chicken in a baking dish. Drizzle over a little honey. Bake at 180°C for 25–30 minutes, basting chicken once or twice during this time. Turn oven to grill for 2–3 minutes to crisp the bacon. Stand for 4–5 minutes before cutting parcels into slices. Arrange chicken slices on serving plates. Serve with vegetables of your choice, or a tossed salad. **Serves 4**.

Cook's Hint: *Thinly sliced prosciutto can be used as an alternative to bacon. It is available from the deli section of most supermarkets.*

warm ginger chicken, crispy noodle and cashew nut salad (top) 58
tandoori chicken salad (bottom) 55

parmesan crumbed chicken

4 single boneless, skinless chicken breasts
1½ cups fresh breadcrumbs (see page 11)
½ cup finely grated parmesan cheese
¼ cup chopped coriander
salt and freshly ground black pepper to season
1 egg, lightly beaten
Rizzoli pure olive oil to drizzle
sweet chilli sauce to serve

Place chicken between 2 sheets of plastic wrap. Pound with a heavy object
(such as a rolling pin) to flatten to an even thickness of 1 cm. Combine
breadcrumbs, cheese, coriander and salt and pepper in a bowl. Dip chicken
into egg, draining off excess. Roll in breadcrumb mixture. Place on a lightly
greased baking tray. Drizzle with a little oil. Bake at 180°C for 20–25
minutes or until chicken is cooked through and golden. Serve with chilli
sauce and a tossed salad. **Serves 4**.

lamb shanks in red wine gravy (top left) 64
citrus and balsamic-glazed chicken (middle) 62
parmesan crumbed chicken (bottom) 61

citrus and balsamic-glazed chicken

½ cup freshly squeezed orange juice (juice of 2 oranges)
¼ cup orange marmalade
¼ cup brown sugar
2 tablespoons Rizzoli balsamic vinegar
8 chicken thighs (bone in), or chicken pieces of your choice
cooked rice to serve

Combine orange juice, marmalade and brown sugar in a saucepan. Stir over a low heat until sugar dissolves. Bring to the boil. Remove from heat and stir in vinegar. Place chicken thighs in a single layer in a baking dish. Pour over glaze and toss to coat. Bake at 190°C for 35–40 minutes or until chicken is cooked through and golden, turning occasionally and spooning glaze over chicken. Serve on a bed of cooked rice. Accompany with a tossed salad or vegetables of your choice. **Serves 4**.

beef stroganoff

500 g rump steak
2 tablespoons butter
1 tablespoon Rizzoli pure olive oil
1 onion, sliced
150 g mushrooms, sliced
¼ cup white wine
¾ cup sour cream
1 tablespoon lemon juice
salt and freshly ground black pepper
cooked Diamond Italian Style fettuccine to serve

Trim fat from meat. Cut meat into thin strips against the grain. Heat butter and oil in a frying pan. Add meat and quickly brown on both sides. Remove from pan and set aside. Add onion and mushrooms to pan. Cook for 5 minutes until onion is clear. Return meat to pan. Add wine and sour cream. Reheat gently. Add lemon juice. Season with salt and pepper to taste, and serve on a bed of fettuccine. **Serves 4**.

lamb shanks
in red wine gravy

½ cup Champion standard grade flour
salt and freshly ground black pepper
8 lamb knuckles*
2 tablespoons Rizzoli pure olive oil
1 onion, finely chopped
1 teaspoon crushed garlic
1½ cups red wine
¼ cup tomato purée
2 cups beef stock
1 tablespoon Edmonds Fielder's cornflour
1 tablespoon water
salt and freshly ground black pepper
3 sprigs rosemary
sprigs of rosemary to garnish

Season flour with salt and pepper. Place in a shallow dish. Trim excess fat from knuckles and discard. Roll in the flour mixture to coat. Heat oil in a large, heavy-based frying pan. Cook 4 knuckles at a time, turning occasionally until browned. Transfer to a roasting pan. Repeat with remaining knuckles. Cover roasting dish and bake at 150°C for 1 hour. Remove dish from oven and pour off any fat. While knuckles are cooking, add onion to the frying pan and cook for 5 minutes until soft. Add garlic, wine, tomato pureé and stock. Mix cornflour to a paste with water. Add to pan, stirring constantly until sauce thickens slightly and comes to the boil. Season. Pour over knuckles. Lay rosemary on top. Cover dish tightly with foil. Bake at 150°C for 2 hours, turning knuckles occasionally. Serve with mashed potato or a combination of mashed potato and mashed kumara. Garnish with sprigs of rosemary. **Serves 4**.

*We used lamb knuckles, which are a trimmed version of lamb shanks — they are easier to fit into a baking dish and look less cumbersome when served.

roast pork loin
with leek and pistachio stuffing

Stuffing
2 tablespoons Rizzoli pure olive oil
1 small leek, thinly sliced and washed
1 cup fresh breadcrumbs (see page 11)
1 small apple, grated
⅓ cup pistachio nuts
1 tablespoon chopped marjoram
salt and freshly ground black pepper to season

2 kg boneless loin of pork
Rizzoli pure olive oil to coat
sea or rock salt to rub
gravy to serve

To make the stuffing, heat oil in a heavy-based frying pan. Cook leeks for 8–10 minutes until soft and all liquid has evaporated. Combine all stuffing ingredients in a bowl. Mix well. Preheat oven to 250°C. Lay pork loin skin-side up on a flat surface. Using a sharp knife, score at 1.5-cm intervals through the skin and just into the layer of fat beneath the skin. Turn loin over. Spread stuffing along the fillet at one end. Roll up and secure at regular intervals with string. Place on a wire rack in a large baking dish. Rub oil then salt into the skin. Bake for 20 minutes until the skin is blistered and golden — crackling has formed. Reduce temperature to 160°C and cook for a further 1½–2 hours (see Cook's Hint below). Stand for 15 minutes before removing string and carving. Serve with gravy. **Serves 8**.

Cook's Hint: *As a general guide, pork takes an hour per kilogram to roast at 160–170°C, including the time for forming the crackling. A meat thermometer is the best way to ensure that the meat is cooked — insert into the thickest part of the meat. At 71°C the meat is medium done and at 76°C it is well done.*

roast chicken
with wild rice and
cashew nut stuffing

Stuffing
½ cup wild rice
1 tablespoon Amco canola oil
1 onion, finely chopped
1 teaspoon crushed garlic
100 g button mushrooms, sliced
½ cup fresh breadcrumbs (see page 11)
½ cup (70 g) roughly chopped roasted cashew nuts
1 egg
salt and freshly ground black pepper to season

1 x no.18 chicken

To make the stuffing, cook rice in boiling water or microwave until tender. Tip into a sieve. Refresh under cold running water. Drain thoroughly. While the rice is cooking, heat oil in a frying pan. Cook onion for 5 minutes until soft. Add garlic and mushrooms and cook for 6–8 minutes until pan is dry. Combine all stuffing ingredients in a bowl. Mix well. Rinse out chicken cavity with cold running water. Drain. Pat chicken dry with paper towels. Spoon stuffing into cavity. Place any leftover stuffing onto a sheet of baking paper, forming a log. Wrap up to enclose and twist ends of paper. Close the chicken cavity using a wooden skewer. Cross legs of chicken and tie with string, so the legs are neatly placed over the chicken. Sit chicken on a rack in a roasting dish. Sprinkle with salt and pepper. Bake at 180°C for 2 hours. About 45 minutes before the end of cooking, place stuffing roll directly on oven rack and bake with chicken. Remove from oven and stand for 5 minutes before carving the chicken. **Serves 5–6**.

Cook's Hint: *To test if chicken is cooked, insert the tip of a sharp knife or metal skewer into the thigh where it joins the body — the juices should run clear.*

roast pork loin with leek and pistachio stuffing (top) 65
roast chicken with wild rice and cashew nut stuffing (middle) 66
roasted root vegetables (bottom) 84

roasted leg of lamb
with garlic and rosemary

5 cloves garlic
1.5–2 kg leg of lamb
12 branches rosemary
salt and freshly ground black pepper

Peel garlic, then cut each clove in half lengthwise. Using a sharp knife, make slits in the surface of the lamb. Insert garlic. Lay 6 branches of the rosemary close together over the base of a roasting dish. Place lamb on top. Season with salt and pepper. Lay remaining branches over lamb. Roast at 160°C, allowing 25 minutes per 500 g. Remove from oven and stand for 10 minutes before carving. Serve with vegetables of your choice. **Serves 6–8**.

Cook's Hint: *Resting the meat after cooking allows the juices to settle and the meat to firm slightly, making carving easier.*

meatloaf with apple, walnut and herb stuffing (top) 75
individual fish pies (bottom) 74

malaysian-style stir-fry

500 g rump steak, thinly sliced
2 tablespoons oyster sauce
2 cloves garlic, crushed
2 tablespoons sesame oil
1 onion, thinly sliced
1 cup cauliflower florets
2 carrots, peeled and thinly sliced
½ red capsicum, thinly sliced
1 stalk celery, thinly sliced
2 teaspoons finely grated root ginger
3 tablespoons hoisin sauce
1 tablespoon sweet chilli sauce
¼ cup water
cooked rice to serve

Combine steak, oyster sauce and garlic in a bowl. Cover and refrigerate for 1 hour. Heat 1 tablespoon of the oil in a large, heavy-based frying pan or wok. Stir-fry meat for 2–3 minutes until just cooked. Remove from pan. Add remaining oil to pan. Add all the vegetables and ginger and stir-fry for 3–4 minutes until tender. Add hoisin and chilli sauces and water. Cook for 1 minute. Return meat to pan. Cook for 2–3 minutes until heated through. Serve on a bed of cooked rice. **Serves 4**.

vegetable, cashew nut and hokkien noodle stir-fry

2 tablespoons Amco canola oil
1 tablespoon finely grated root ginger
1 teaspoon crushed garlic
2 carrots, thinly sliced
1 small head broccoli, cut into small florets
100 g snow peas
2 heads shang hai choy*, leaves separated
3 spring onions, sliced
½ cup roasted, salted cashew nuts
¼ cup soy sauce
1 tablespoon sweet chilli sauce
400 g hokkien noodles*

Heat oil in a wok or large heavy-based frying pan. Cook ginger and garlic for 2–3 minutes. Add carrots and broccoli and stir-fry for 3–4 minutes. Add snow peas, shang hai choy, spring onions and cashew nuts and stir-fry for 2 minutes. Add soy sauce and chilli sauce and stir through vegetables. Add noodles to pan and stir-fry for about 2 minutes until heated through. Serve immediately. **Serves 3–4**.

*Shang hai choy is a green leafy Asian vegetable. It is similar to bok choy, but has a smaller leaf. It can be found in the fruit and vegetable section of selected supermarkets or from fruit and vegetable suppliers.

*Hokkien noodles are wheat-based Chinese noodles used in Asian cuisine. They are ideal for use in stir-fries, soups and salads and can be purchased from the Asian or noodle section of most supermarkets.

Cook's Hint: *Because the cooking process is very quick for this recipe and requires constant stir-frying, have all the vegetables prepared and ingredients measured out prior to commencing cooking.*

pasta bake
with ham and mushrooms

250 g Diamond pasta shapes, e.g. penne or rigati
2 tablespoons Rizzoli pure olive oil
1 onion, finely chopped
1 teaspoon crushed garlic
150 g button mushrooms, sliced
1 tablespoon grainy mustard
4 slices ham, chopped
1½ cups milk
½ cup cream
½ cup freshly grated parmesan cheese
4 eggs, lightly beaten
salt and freshly ground black pepper to season
1 cup grated tasty cheddar cheese

Cook pasta according to instructions on packet. Tip into a sieve and refresh under cold running water. Drain thoroughly. Heat oil in a heavy-based frying pan. Cook onion for 4–5 minutes until soft. Add garlic, mushrooms and mustard and cook for a further 6–8 minutes or until pan is dry. Combine pasta, mushroom mixture and ham in a bowl. Spread over the base of a large, greased baking dish. Whisk together milk, cream, parmesan, eggs and salt and pepper. Pour over pasta. Sprinkle over cheddar cheese. Bake at 180°C for 35–40 minutes or until firm to the touch. Serve with a tossed salad. **Serves 4**.

Cook's Hint: *Diced, cooked rindless bacon can be substituted for the ham.*

pumpkin and feta lasagne

150 g Diamond lasagne
1 cup firmly packed, grated, peeled pumpkin
250 g cottage cheese
100 g feta cheese, diced
1 spring onion, chopped
2 eggs
½ teaspoon ground nutmeg
salt and freshly ground black pepper to season
500 g bottled pasta sauce
1½ cups grated tasty cheddar cheese

Cook lasagne according to packet instructions. Tip into a sieve and cool under cold running water. Drain. Combine pumpkin, cottage cheese, feta, spring onion, eggs and nutmeg in a bowl. Mix well. Season to taste. Spread half of the pumpkin mixture over the base of a greased ovenproof dish. Cover with a single layer of lasagne. Spread over half the pasta sauce. Repeat the layers once more, ending with the pasta sauce. Sprinkle over cheese. Bake at 190°C for 20–25 minutes. **Serves 4**.

seafood risotto

about 1.5 litres chicken or fish stock
¼ cup Rizzoli extra virgin olive oil
1 onion, finely chopped
2 cloves garlic, crushed
500 g arborio rice
1 cup dry white wine
250 g firm white fish fillets, cut into chunks
16 scallops (optional)
12 marinated mussels, drained
100 g cooked prawns or shrimps
½ cup freshly grated parmesan cheese
finely grated zest of 1 lemon
juice of 1 lemon
3 tablespoons chopped dill or parsley
salt and freshly ground black pepper to season

Bring stock to the boil in a saucepan. Heat oil in a heavy-based, deep-sided frying pan. Cook onion for 5 minutes until soft. Add garlic and rice and stir over a low heat for 2–3 minutes to toast the rice. Add ½ cup of wine and cook for 1 minute. Ladle over sufficient boiling stock to just cover the rice. Cook, stirring frequently, adding more stock to cover the rice as the liquid is absorbed. (This will take about 18 minutes.) Three to 4 minutes before the rice is cooked, bring remaining wine to the boil in a saucepan. Add fish chunks and cook for 1 minute, turning once. Add scallops, cook for a further minute until fish and scallops just turn white. The seafood will not be completely cooked at this stage. Remove from heat. Drain liquid from pan. Add all seafood, parmesan, lemon zest and juice to cooked rice. Toss gently to combine. Cover pan and stand for 3–4 minutes. Stir in dill or parsley. Season to taste with salt and pepper. Serve immediately on warm plates. **Serves 4**.

sausage, chicken
and bacon cassoulet

300 g dried haricot beans
2 x 400 g cans tomatoes in juice, chopped
1 tablespoon Dijon mustard
1 teaspoon crushed garlic
2 bay leaves
2 onions, thinly sliced
salt and freshly ground black pepper to season
4 sausages
4 chicken pieces
4 rashers rindless bacon, chopped

Place the beans in a bowl. Cover to 3 cm above the level of the beans with cold water. Leave to soak overnight. Drain the beans. Place in a saucepan. Cover with water and bring to the boil. Simmer for 25 minutes. Drain. Combine tomatoes, mustard, garlic, bay leaves, onions and salt and pepper in a bowl. Layer sausages, chicken, bacon, beans and tomato mixture in a large casserole dish. Cover and bake at 160°C for 3 hours until meats and beans are cooked. Remove bay leaves. Adjust seasoning to taste. Serve with seasonal vegetables. **Serves 4–5**.

Cook's Hint: *A cassoulet is a traditional French one-dish meal of white beans layered with meats such as sausage, goose and duck. The long, slow cooking results in a delicious meal. Note that the beans need to be soaked overnight.*

individual fish pies

6 large potatoes, peeled
large knob of butter
milk to mash
salt and freshly ground black pepper to season
1 small head broccoli, cut into florets
2 tablespoons butter
2 tablespoons Champion standard grade flour
1 cup milk
500 g smoked fish, flaked*
1 tablespoon chopped parsley
2 hard-boiled eggs, shelled and quartered

Cut potatoes into 6–8 pieces then microwave or boil until tender. Drain thoroughly. Add butter and sufficient milk to mash to a soft consistency. Season. Line the bases of 4 greased 1½-cup-capacity ramekins with a 2-cm depth of mashed potato. Cook broccoli in microwave or steam until just tender. Tip into a sieve and refresh under cold running water. Drain. Melt second measure of butter in a saucepan. Add flour and stir constantly for 2 minutes. Remove from heat. Gradually add milk, stirring continuously. Return pan to heat. Stir constantly until sauce thickens and comes to the boil. Remove from heat. Gently fold through broccoli, fish, parsley and egg. Divide fish mixture between ramekins. Cover with remaining potato. Bake at 190°C for 15 minutes or until golden. **Serves 4**.

*A 425 g can of drained, flaked smoked fish can be used as an alternative to the fresh smoked fish.

meatloaf
with apple, walnut and herb stuffing

Stuffing
1½ cups fresh breadcrumbs (see page 11)
2 spring onions, finely sliced
1 stalk celery, finely chopped
¾ cup chopped walnuts
1 apple, grated (skin included)
¼ cup chopped parsley
2 cloves garlic, crushed
1 egg
salt and freshly ground black pepper to season

Meatloaf
1 egg
500 g lean minced beef (or lamb)
500 g quality sausage meat
1 onion, finely chopped
2 tablespoons tomato paste
relish or chutney to serve

To make the stuffing, combine all ingredients and mix well. To make the meatloaf, combine all ingredients and mix well. Lay a sheet of foil on a flat surface. Turn meat onto foil. Pat into a 30-cm x 22-cm rectangle. Lay stuffing along one edge of meat. Using the foil to help, roll meat around the stuffing to enclose. Slide meatloaf off foil into a greased metal baking dish. Bake at 180°C for 1 hour. Remove from oven and stand for 10 minutes before slicing. Serve with relish or chutney and a tossed salad. **Serves 6**.

Cook's Hint: *This meatloaf is also delicious served cold.*

hearty beef goulash

1 kg braising steak, e.g. blade or skirt
2 tablespoons Champion standard grade flour
2 teaspoons paprika
salt and freshly ground black pepper to season
2 tablespoons Amco canola oil
2 onions, thinly sliced
1 teaspoon crushed garlic
400 g can tomatoes in juice, roughly chopped
2 teaspoons Edmonds Fielder's cornflour
1 tablespoon water
cooked Diamond Italian Style fettuccine to serve
chopped parsley to garnish

Trim fat from meat and discard. Cut meat into bite-size pieces. Combine flour, paprika and salt and pepper in a bowl. Add meat and toss until evenly coated. Heat 1 tablespoon of the oil in a frying pan. Cook onion and garlic for about 5 minutes until soft. Transfer to a casserole dish. Add remaining oil to pan. Cook meat over a high heat for 4–5 minutes until browned. Transfer to casserole dish. Pour tomatoes over meat and stir well. Cover dish and bake at 160°C for 2¼ hours, or until meat is tender. Mix cornflour to a paste with water. Stir into meat. Cover and cook for a further 15 minutes. Serve on a bed of cooked fettuccine. Garnish with chopped parsley. **Serves 4**.

lamb and apricot tagine

1 cup dried apricots
1 cup boiling water
1 tablespoon Champion standard grade flour
1 teaspoon cinnamon
1 teaspoon coriander
1 teaspoon cumin
salt and freshly ground black pepper to season
750 g lean lamb, diced
1 tablespoon Amco canola oil
2 onions, thinly sliced
2 teaspoons Edmonds Fielder's cornflour
1 tablespoon water
¼ cup flaked almonds to garnish
coriander leaves to garnish

Soak apricots in the boiling water for 30 minutes. Combine flour, spices and salt and pepper in a bowl. Add lamb and toss until evenly coated. Transfer to a casserole dish. Heat oil in a frying pan. Cook onion for 5 minutes until soft. Transfer to casserole dish. Add apricots and water. Stir well. Cover dish and bake at 180°C for 1 hour, until meat is tender. Mix cornflour to a paste with water and stir into meat mixture. Cover and cook for a further 15 minutes. Garnish with almonds and coriander leaves. Serve with couscous or mashed potatoes and seasonal vegetables of your choice. **Serves 4**.

osso buco

¼ cup Champion standard grade flour
⅛ teaspoon salt
½ teaspoon freshly ground black pepper
4 pieces beef or veal shin on the bone
3 tablespoons Amco canola oil
2 onions, sliced
2 carrots, peeled and sliced
3 sticks celery, sliced
3 cloves garlic, finely chopped
¾ cup dry white wine
500 ml beef stock
400 g can tomatoes in juice, roughly chopped
1 sprig rosemary
3 tablespoons chopped parsley
salt and freshly ground black pepper

Combine flour, salt and pepper. Spread out on a flat plate. Roll meat in the seasoned flour to coat, shaking off any excess. Heat oil in a large, heavy-based saucepan. Cook the meat, 2 pieces at a time, turning occasionally until brown all over. Remove from pan and set aside. Add onions, carrots, celery and garlic to the pan, cooking 4–5 minutes until the onion is translucent. Add leftover flour to the pan, stirring constantly for 2 minutes. Remove pan from heat, gradually add wine, then stock, stirring to incorporate. Add tomatoes and rosemary. Return pan to the heat, stirring constantly until sauce thickens and comes to the boil. Return shin on the bone to the pan. Cover and simmer for 1½ hours, turning meat occasionally. Remove rosemary sprig. Stir in parsley. Season to taste with salt and pepper. To serve, transfer to a warm serving dish. Accompany with risotto, pasta or mashed potatoes. **Serves 4**.

vegetables

Vegetables have come a long way

since the days of overcooked,

tasteless cabbage and soggy mashed

potatoes. It only takes a bit of flair

and a few minutes to produce any of

these inviting vegetable dishes, which

are packed full of vitamins. These

recipes are ideal for vegetarians and

make great accompaniments to any

chicken or fish dish. They are also

just as good served on their own as a

light meal.

rosemary and parmesan potatoes

2 tablespoons Rizzoli extra virgin olive oil
6 potatoes, scrubbed and diced
1 teaspoon crushed garlic
½ cup finely grated parmesan cheese
3 tablespoons chopped rosemary
rock salt (or regular salt) to sprinkle

Preheat oven to 220°C. Heat oil in a heavy-based frying pan. Cook potatoes and garlic for 4–5 minutes, stirring frequently, until light golden. Transfer to a shallow baking dish. Scatter cheese, rosemary and a little salt over potatoes. Cook for 15 minutes until golden. **Serves 4, as a vegetable accompaniment to a main meal**.

stir-fried cabbage
with cumin seeds

2 tablespoons Rizzoli pure olive oil
2 tablespoons cumin seeds
½ medium-sized cabbage*, thinly sliced

Heat oil in a large frying pan. Add seeds and stir-fry for 30 seconds. Add cabbage and stir-fry for 2–3 minutes until just tender. Serve immediately. **Serves 4 as a vegetable accompaniment to a main meal**.

*A combination of red and green cabbage can be used.

ginger sesame beans

2 teaspoons sesame oil
300 g green beans, ends trimmed
2 teaspoons finely grated root ginger
2 tablespoons toasted sesame seeds (see page 12)

Heat oil in a heavy-based frying pan or wok. Stir-fry beans and ginger for 3–4 minutes until tender. Sprinkle over sesame seeds, tossing to coat. **Serves 4 as a vegetable accompaniment to a main meal**.

caramelised parsnips

400 g parsnips (4 medium size), peeled
¼ cup freshly squeezed orange juice (juice of 1 orange)
2 tablespoons butter
2 tablespoons brown sugar
finely chopped chives to garnish

Cut parsnips into even-sized lengths. Fill a saucepan with water to a level of 2 cm and bring to the boil. Add parsnips and cook for 2 minutes. Remove from the saucepan and drain. Combine orange juice, butter and brown sugar in the saucepan. Stir over a low heat until butter has melted and sugar has dissolved. Add parsnips and cook over a low heat, uncovered, for about 12 minutes, stirring occasionally, until tender and golden. Garnish with chives. **Serves 4 as a vegetable accompaniment to a main meal**.

roasted root vegetables

**selection of root vegetables, e.g. potatoes, kumara, pumpkin,
  carrots, parsnips**
Rizzoli extra virgin olive oil to cook
rock salt (or regular salt) to sprinkle

Scrub or peel vegetables, as desired, then cut into chunks or lengths of approximately the same size. Preheat oven to 200°C. Pour a little oil over the base of a roasting dish. Heat dish in oven for 2–3 minutes. Add vegetables and toss to combine. Sprinkle over a little salt. Roast for 15–30 minutes (depending on the size of the vegetable chunks) until vegetables are tender and golden. If the vegetables are tender, but not as golden as you would like, turn oven to grill and cook vegetables to the desired colour.

desserts

Desserts are the ultimate in comfort

food. The sweet treats featured in

this book offer a variety of flavours

and are worth the time spent

choosing and putting them together.

Whether your choice is fresh fruit,

dried fruits, nuts or chocolate, there

is something for everyone here.

Enjoy!

moist date pudding
with butterscotch sauce

1½ cups halved pitted dates
1½ cups water
1 teaspoon Edmonds baking soda
150 g butter, softened
1 cup brown sugar
⅓ cup golden syrup
2 eggs
1 teaspoon vanilla essence
2 cups Champion standard grade flour
1 teaspoon Edmonds baking powder

Butterscotch Sauce
50 g butter
1 cup brown sugar
2 tablespoons golden syrup
¼ cup cream

Combine dates and water in a saucepan. Bring to the boil. Remove from heat and allow to cool to lukewarm. Stir in baking soda. Beat butter and sugar until light and creamy. Warm golden syrup slightly, then add to butter mixture. Beat well. Add eggs one at a time, beating well after each addition. Beat in essence. Sift flour and baking powder. Fold dry ingredients and date mixture alternately into butter mixture. Transfer to a greased 22-cm-round cake tin that has had the base lined with baking paper. Bake at 180°C for 50–55 minutes or until cake springs back when lightly pressed. Stand for 10 minutes before turning out and cutting into wedges. Serve warm, accompanied by Butterscotch Sauce. To make the sauce, melt butter in a small saucepan. Add sugar and golden syrup and stir until sugar dissolves. Add cream and stir constantly until sauce almost comes to the boil. **Serves 8.**

pear and ginger upside-down pudding (top right) 87
moist date pudding with butterscotch sauce (bottom right) 86
individual peach and coffee custard trifles (left) 88

pear and ginger upside-down pudding

3 tablespoons melted butter
½ cup brown sugar
2 tablespoons freshly squeezed orange juice
2 firm, ripe pears, peeled, quartered and cored

Batter
150 g butter, softened
1 cup brown sugar
2 eggs
2½ cups Champion standard grade flour
½ teaspoon Edmonds baking powder
3 teaspoons ground ginger
1 teaspoon Edmonds baking soda
1 cup warm milk
whipped cream or ice cream to serve

Grease the sides of a 23-cm-round cake tin. Combine butter, brown sugar and orange juice. Mix well. Spread over the base of tin. Cut each pear quarter into 4 slices. Arrange in an overlapping pattern over the base of the baking tin. To make the batter, beat butter and brown sugar until light and creamy. Add eggs one at a time, beating well after each addition. Sift flour, baking powder and ginger. Dissolve baking soda in milk. Fold dry ingredients and milk alternately into butter mixture. Spoon over top of pears. Bake for 50–55 minutes or until a skewer inserted in centre of cake comes out clean. Stand for 5 minutes, then invert onto a serving plate. Serve warm with whipped cream or ice cream. **Serves 8.**

Cook's Hint: *This pudding is also delicious cold. Stored in an airtight container, it will keep for up to 2 days.*

chocolate brownies (left) 89
mascarpone flans with pecan praline (right) 92

individual peach and coffee custard trifles

3 tablespoons Edmonds custard powder
1½ cups milk
1 tablespoon instant coffee
¼ cup sugar
½ cup cream, whipped
225 g Ernest Adams unfilled sponge
2 x 415 g cans peaches in light syrup
sprigs of mint to garnish

To make the Coffee Custard, mix the custard powder to a paste with ¼ cup of the milk. Place remaining milk in a saucepan and stir in coffee. Gradually add custard mixture, stirring constantly. Stir in sugar. Stir over a medium heat until custard thickens. Remove from heat. Transfer to a bowl and cover surface of custard with plastic wrap to prevent a skin forming. Refrigerate until cold. Fold whipped cream into custard. Cut sponge into small cubes and divide between 4 individual serving glasses or dishes. Drain peaches, reserving juice. Spoon sufficient juice over sponge to moisten. Divide peach slices between the serving glasses, reserving 8 slices for garnish. Top with custard. Cover and refrigerate for at least 2 hours. Just before serving, garnish with reserved peach slices and sprigs of mint. **Serves 4**.

chocolate brownies

250 g butter, chopped
200 g dark chocolate, chopped
2 cups sugar
4 eggs, lightly beaten
1 teaspoon vanilla essence
1 cup Champion standard grade flour
½ teaspoon Edmonds baking powder
½ cup cocoa
icing sugar to dust (optional)
vanilla ice cream or whipped cream to serve

Combine butter and chocolate in a saucepan. Stir constantly over a low heat until melted and smooth. Remove from heat and transfer mixture to a large bowl. Stir in sugar. Add eggs and essence and beat with a wooden spoon until combined. Sift flour, baking powder and cocoa. Stir into chocolate mixture. Transfer to a greased 25-cm x 20-cm baking tin that has had the base lined with baking paper. Bake at 180°C for about 50 minutes or until firm to touch, with cracks appearing on the surface. Cool in tin. Turn onto a chopping board. Trim off edges and cut into triangles. Arrange on serving plates. If desired, dust with icing sugar. Serve with ice cream or whipped cream.

pear, apple and ginger crumble with custard

3 apples, peeled, quartered, cored and sliced
3 pears, peeled, quartered, cored and sliced
³/₄ cup brown sugar
1 teaspoon cinnamon
1 tablespoon water

Crumble
2 cups Fleming's rolled oats
1 cup Champion standard grade flour
1 cup brown sugar
1¹/₂ teaspoons ground ginger
100 g butter, melted

custard to serve

Arrange fruit in a large ovenproof baking dish. Sprinkle over sugar, cinnamon and water. Combine crumble ingredients in a bowl. Mix well. Sprinkle over fruit. Press lightly with the back of a spoon. Bake at 180°C for 45 minutes. Serve with custard. **Serves 6–8**.

individual fruit
bread and butter puddings

8 slices Quality Bakers thick-cut fruit bread
softened butter to spread
½ cup raisins
2 eggs
¾ cup milk
½ cup cream
¼ cup sugar
1 teaspoon vanilla essence
nutmeg to sprinkle
a little brown sugar to sprinkle

Grease four 10-cm-diameter ramekins. Line bases with baking paper. Using a 10-cm-diameter biscuit cutter, stamp a circle from each slice of bread. Lightly butter both sides of the bread rounds. Place a bread round in the base of each ramekin. Sprinkle with raisins. Cover with remaining bread rounds. Whisk together eggs, milk, cream, sugar and essence. Gradually pour egg mixture over bread. Press down on bread lightly with the back of a spoon to ensure it is soaked. Sprinkle lightly with nutmeg. Stand for 10 minutes. Place ramekins in a baking dish. Pour sufficient boiling water into baking dish to come halfway up the sides of the ramekins. Bake at 180°C for 25 minutes or until puddings are set. Preheat grill. Run a knife around the edge of each ramekin. Turn puddings onto a baking tray. Sprinkle lightly with brown sugar. Grill for 2–3 minutes or until sugar melts. **Serves 4**.

Cook's Hint: *For a decadent pudding, replace the essence with 1 tablespoon of whisky or rum.*

mascarpone flans
with pecan praline

6 sheets pre-rolled Ernest Adams butter crust pastry

Filling
2 teaspoons gelatine
1 tablespoon cold water
¼ cup liquid honey
1 teaspoon vanilla essence
250 g mascarpone*
½ cup cream, whipped

Pecan Praline
½ cup pecan nuts
½ cup sugar

Using a 20-cm-round guide, cut a circle from each sheet of pastry. Discard trimmings. Line six 10-cm-round loose-bottomed flan tins. Prick bases several times with a fork. Refrigerate for 15 minutes. Cover base of pastry cases with baking paper. Fill with dried beans, rice or baking blind material. Bake at 180°C for 12 minutes. Remove baking blind material and bake for a further 8–10 minutes until golden. Cool. To make the filling, sprinkle gelatine over the cold water. Place over a bowl of hot water and stir until gelatine dissolves. Add honey and essence and beat into mascarpone with a wooden spoon. Fold in cream. Spoon filling into pastry shell, spreading evenly. Cover and refrigerate for at least 2 hours before serving. Just before serving, scatter Pecan Praline over flans. To make the praline, place sugar in a small saucepan. Stir over a low heat until the sugar melts. Add pecan nuts. Increase heat slightly and, watching closely and stirring occasionally, allow the mixture to turn a light caramel colour. Spread mixture thinly on a greased baking tray. Allow to cool, then break into pieces. Either pulse to a coarse crumb in a food processor fitted with a metal blade or chop with a large sharp knife. **Serves 6**.

*Mascarpone is Italian in origin and is used extensively for desserts. It can be found in the refrigerated section of most supermarkets.

lemon tart

Sweet Shortcrust Pastry
  (makes 200 g or use 200 g Ernest Adams butter crust pastry)
1 cup Champion standard grade flour
75 g butter
¼ cup sugar
1 egg yolk
1 tablespoon water

Filling
3 eggs
¼ cup lemon juice
1 tablespoon grated lemon zest
½ cup caster sugar
¾ cup cream

lemon zest to garnish

To make the pastry, sift flour. Cut in butter until it resembles fine breadcrumbs. Stir in sugar. Add egg yolk and water. Mix to a stiff dough. Cover with plastic wrap and chill for 30 minutes before using. Roll pastry out on a lightly floured surface to line a 20-cm-round loose-bottom flan tin. Prick base several times with a fork. Refrigerate for 10 minutes. Cover base of flan tin with baking paper. Fill with dried beans, rice or baking blind material. Bake blind at 190°C for 15 minutes. Remove baking blind material and cook for a further 3 minutes. To make the filling, beat eggs, lemon juice, zest and sugar until combined. Lightly beat in cream. Pour into pastry shell. Bake at 190°C for 5 minutes, then reduce temperature to 150°C and cook for a further 20–25 minutes or until tart is set. Garnish with lemon zest. Serve warm or cold. **Serves 6**.

rustic rhubarb
and apple tarts

2 medium Granny Smith apples
250 g (3 stalks) rhubarb, washed
½ cup brown sugar
2 tablespoons Champion standard grade flour
2 teaspoons grated lemon zest
4 sheets pre-rolled Ernest Adams butter crust pastry
lemon zest (optional) to garnish
whipped cream to serve

Peel, core and quarter apples. Cut into 1.5-cm chunks. Cut rhubarb into 1.5-cm lengths. Combine fruit, sugar, flour and zest in a bowl. Mix well. Using a 20-cm-round guide, cut a circle from each sheet of pastry. Discard trimmings. Pile one quarter of the fruit mixture onto the pastry, leaving a 4-cm border. Working around the filling, gather up the pastry, pleating it in one direction and folding the pastry onto itself in regularly spaced pleats. Transfer to a baking tray. Repeat with remaining pastry and fruit, to give 4 tarts. Refrigerate for 15 minutes. Bake at 180°C for 30 minutes or until fruit is tender and pastry is golden. Stand for 10 minutes before serving. Garnish with lemon zest. Serve with whipped cream.

Cook's Hint: *This recipe makes 4 large, individual tarts. For a more modest serving, halve the recipe to make 2 tarts and cut in half to serve.*

quick dessert ideas
with irvines pies

Irvines Family Fruit Pies are a convenient dessert option. Keep a selection of these delicious fruit-filled pies (Apple, Apricot or Apple and Blackberry) on hand and you will have an instant dessert the whole family will enjoy. Great too, for unexpected dinner guests. Follow the instructions on the pack for warming, then serve with one of the following:

- Hot custard made with Edmonds Custard Powder. For a grown-ups' custard, try adding a splash of liqueur, e.g. Grand Marnier.
- Mascarpone
- Whipped cream
- Ice cream — if time permits, try this delicious, simple homemade Vanilla Ice Cream

vanilla ice cream
3 eggs, separated
½ cup caster sugar
2 teaspoons vanilla extract
300 ml cream, lightly whipped

Place egg yolks, sugar and vanilla in a bowl. Using an electric mixer, beat on high speed until thick and pale. In a separate bowl, beat egg whites until soft peaks form. Fold cream, followed by whites, into yolk mixture. Transfer to a plastic container. Cover and freeze for at least 4 hours, until firm. **Makes about 1½ litres**.

Cook's Hint: *Vanilla extract is preferable to vanilla essence as it gives a true vanilla flavour.*

winter fruit salad

2 cups freshly squeezed orange juice (about 8 oranges)
½ cup water
⅓ cup liquid honey
2 cinnamon sticks
⅓ cup brandy (optional)
200 g dried apricots
150 g dried figs
100 g pitted prunes
whipped cream or ice cream or yoghurt to serve

Strain orange juice through a fine sieve into a saucepan. Add water, honey and 1 cinnamon stick. Stir over a low heat until honey dissolves. Bring to the boil, reduce heat and simmer for 45 minutes. Remove cinnamon stick and discard. Stir in brandy. Pack dried fruit and remaining cinnamon stick into a clean sterilised jar. Pour syrup over fruit. Cover jar tightly with a lid. Store in the refrigerator. (The fruit salad will keep for up to 2 months stored in the fridge.) Serve with whipped cream, ice cream or yoghurt. **Serves 4–5**.

Cook's Hint: *The homemade Vanilla Ice Cream on page 95 is a great accompaniment to this fruit salad.*

little sweet treats

These delicious little morsels make an ideal

accompaniment to a well-deserved mid-

morning cup of tea or coffee, or can be

served with after-dinner coffee instead of

(or after) desserts. Make a double batch to

ensure you always have something on hand

when friends drop in unexpectedly.

lemon shortbread shapes

125 g butter, softened
½ cup icing sugar
1 tablespoon finely grated lemon zest
1¼ cups Champion standard grade flour
½ cup Edmonds Fielder's cornflour

Cream butter and icing sugar until light and fluffy. Beat in zest. Sift flour and cornflour. Mix sifted ingredients into creamed mixture. Gather dough together and transfer to a lightly floured surface. Knead for 1 minute. Roll dough out to a thickness of 7.5 mm. Using a small biscuit cutter, stamp shapes from the dough and place on a greased baking tray. Re-roll dough and continue stamping out shapes until all the dough is used. Bake at 160°C for 15–20 minutes or until pale golden. Transfer to wire racks to cool. Store in an airtight container.

almond chocolate truffles

250 g dark chocolate, chopped
25 g butter, chopped
½ cup cream
1 tablespoon Amaretto liqueur (optional)
¼ cup ground almonds
finely chopped, toasted blanched almonds
sifted cocoa or melted dark chocolate to coat

Put chocolate and butter in the top of a double boiler or heatproof bowl. Place over simmering water. Stir constantly until chocolate melts and the mixture is smooth. Remove from heat. Stir in cream, liqueur and ground almonds. Cover and refrigerate for several hours until firm. Roll teaspoonfuls of mixture into balls. Place in a single layer on a plate. Cover with and refrigerate for 1 hour. To coat truffles, roll in almonds or cocoa, or dip in melted chocolate using a dipping stick or 2 teaspoons and allowing excess chocolate to drain off. Place on a sheet of foil and allow to dry. Store truffles in a covered container in a cool place. **Makes 42 truffles**.

Cook's Hint: *If not using Amaretto liqueur, then add a couple of drops of almond essence.*

florentines

1½ cups cornflakes
½ cup sliced almonds
½ cup chopped red glacé cherries
½ cup sultanas
¼ cup mixed peel
2 tablespoons finely chopped crystallised ginger
2 tablespoons Champion standard grade flour
½ cup sweetened condensed milk
125 g dark chocolate, melted (see page 12)

Combine cornflakes, almonds, cherries, sultanas, peel and ginger in a bowl. Mix well. Sprinkle over flour, then mix to combine. Stir in condensed milk. Line baking trays with baking paper. Place heaped tablespoons of mixture 4 cm apart on baking paper, then spread out with the back of the spoon to form 5-cm-diameter circles. Bake at 180°C for 10 minutes or until golden. Stand for 3–4 minutes before transferring to wire racks to cool. Spread the flat side of each Florentine with melted chocolate. Allow to partially set, then use a fork to mark lines on the chocolate. Allow to set. Store in an airtight container in a cool place. **Makes 26**.

Cook's Hint: *It is vital that the Florentines are left to stand before being removed from the baking trays, as this allows them to firm up.*

quick chocolate walnut fudge

3½ cups icing sugar
¼ cup cocoa
100 g butter, chopped
1 teaspoon vanilla essence
¼ cup cream
½ cup roughly chopped walnuts

Lightly grease a shallow 20-cm-square baking dish. Sift icing sugar and cocoa into a large microwave-proof bowl. Make a well in the centre and drop in butter, essence and cream. Cover lightly with baking paper. Microwave on high power for 1½ minutes. Add walnuts and beat well with a wooden spoon. Pour into dish and spread evenly. Cool. Cover and refrigerate until firm. Cut into small squares.

Cook's Hint: *If desired, cut fudge into shapes using small biscuit cutters.*

tiny lemon curd tartlets

Lemon Curd Filling
1 tablespoon finely grated lemon zest
¼ cup lemon juice
2 eggs, lightly beaten
50 g butter
¼ cup caster sugar

3 sheets pre-rolled Ernest Adams butter crust pastry

To make the Lemon Curd Filling, combine lemon zest and juice, eggs, butter and sugar in the top of a double boiler or in a heatproof bowl. Place over simmering water. Stir constantly until sugar dissolves and curd thickens. Remove from heat. Cover and cool. Using a 6-cm-round biscuit cutter, stamp circles from pastry. Use to line mini muffin tins. Prick bases with a fork. Freeze for 5 minutes. Bake at 180°C for 10 minutes until golden. Remove pastry cases from tins and cool on a wire rack. Just before serving, fill with Lemon Curd Filling. **Makes 24 tartlets**.

Cook's Hint: *The pastry shells and Lemon Curd Filling can be prepared up to 2 days in advance. Keep pastry shells in an airtight container. Cover Lemon Curd Filling and refrigerate.*

hazelnut biscotti

2 cups Champion standard grade flour
2 teaspoons Edmonds baking powder
pinch of salt
³/₄ cup caster sugar
2 teaspoons vanilla essence
3 eggs
½ cup chopped, roasted hazelnuts (see page 12)

Sift flour, baking powder and salt into a bowl. Stir in caster sugar. Lightly beat essence and eggs together. Stir egg mixture and hazelnuts into dry ingredients, mixing until well combined. The dough should be firm. Add more flour if necessary. Shape into a log about 30 cm long. Place on greased oven tray and flatten log with the palm of your hand. Bake at 180°C for 35 minutes or until cooked. Cool for 10 minutes, then cut log into 1-cm slices on the diagonal. Place slices on an oven tray. Bake at 150°C for 20 minutes or until biscotti are dry and crisp. Store in an airtight container. **Makes about 30 biscotti**.

Cook's Hint: *Twice baked (to remove nearly all the moisture) these hard Italian biscuits were originally made to take on long voyages as they did not go stale.*

mini orange
melting moments

200 g butter, softened
3/4 cup icing sugar
finely grated zest of 1 medium orange
1 cup Champion standard grade flour
1 cup Edmonds Fielder's cornflour
1/2 teaspoon Edmonds baking powder

Orange Icing
1 cup icing sugar
1 teaspoon butter
1 tablespoon freshly squeezed orange juice
a little boiling water to mix

Cream butter and icing sugar until light and fluffy. Beat in orange zest. Sift flour, cornflour and baking powder. Add to creamed mixture. Mix well. Take level teaspoons of mixture and shape into small balls. Place on a greased oven tray. Flatten slightly with a floured fork. Bake at 180°C for 12–15 minutes. Cool on wire racks. To make the Orange Icing, place icing sugar, butter and orange juice in a bowl. Add sufficient water to mix to a spreadable consistency. Sandwich 2 biscuits together with Orange Icing. **Makes 32**.

menu
ideas

breakfast or brunch menu

The following menu would be suitable for a breakfast or brunch occasion. Keeping last-minute preparation and cooking to a minimum enables the host to enjoy the meal, too!

Chunky Honey Toasted Muesli (page 14)
Serve with seasonal fresh fruit and Greek yoghurt.

❂

Blueberry Cream Cheese Loaf (page 32)

❂

Brioche (page 36)
Serve with Lemon Curd (page 20).

❂

Eggs Benedict (page 24)

Hints
- Plan beverages to accompany the menu, e.g. freshly squeezed orange juice (or other fruit juice of your choice), freshly brewed tea and coffee and have a jug of chilled water in the refrigerator.
- To minimise rushing around before breakfast guests arrive, set the table the night before, including cutlery and crockery.

Prepare Ahead
- Chunky Honey Toasted Muesli can be made up to a week in advance.
- Blueberry Cream Cheese Loaf — make the day before required.
- Brioche — prepare the dough the evening before, as per instructions given in the recipe.
- Lemon Curd — can be made, and kept refrigerated, up to 1 month in advance if desired.
- Eggs Benedict — make the Hollandaise Sauce the day before.

On the Day
- Cook brioche.
- Cook Eggs Benedict to order.

lunch menu

On the whole, a light lunch will be more appreciated by guests than a heavy meal, allowing them to function for the remainder of the day! The following menu can be prepared in about 1 hour — very much a maximum effect for minimum effort affair!

Warm Ginger Chicken, Crispy Noodle and Cashew Nut Salad (page 58)

❂

Lemon Tart (page 93)

❂

Tea/Coffee with Quick Chocolate Walnut Fudge (page 101)

Hints
- Place a jug of water in the refrigerator to chill. Serve with lemon or lime slices.
- For a special occasion, choose a light white wine to accompany the salad. A Pinot Gris or Riesling would be a good choice.

Prepare Ahead
- Prepare chicken for the salad the day before.
- Make dressing for the salad the day before.
- Make Quick Chocolate Walnut Fudge the day before.

On the Day
- Marinate chicken for salad.
- Make Lemon Tart.
- Prepare all salad ingredients and cook chicken.

dinner menu

The following menu is ideal for a mid-week dinner, with quick preparation requirements. If time is of the essence, make the Chocolate Brownies the day before.

Antipasto Platter with Quality Bakers Turkish Bread
— purchase a selection of items from the supermarket deli and arrange on a large platter. Accompany with sliced Quality Bakers Turkish bread. Examples are: olives, sundried or semi-dried tomatoes, roasted capsicums, marinated feta cheese, artichoke hearts, cherry tomatoes, sliced salami, pastrami or prosciutto.

❀

Blue Cheese and Walnut Stuffed Chicken Breasts (page 60)

❀

Rosemary and Parmesan Potatoes (page 80)
Cook after the chicken — keep chicken warm while cooking the potatoes.

❀

Tossed Salad
— mesculin mixes are a convenient salad base. Add sliced cucumber, sliced avocado, sliced spring onions and cherry or quartered regular tomatoes. Toss through Vinaigrette Dressing (page 12).

❀

Chocolate Brownies (page 89)

Prepare Ahead
- Flatten the chicken breasts according to recipe instructions.
- Make the stuffing for the chicken.
- Make Chocolate Brownies.
- Make Vinaigrette Dressing.

On the Day
- Complete chicken breasts and cook.
- Cook potatoes.
- Make Tossed Salad.
- Assemble Antipasto Platter.
- Whip cream if serving with Chocolate Brownies.

Platter from left to right:
almond chocolate truffles 99
mini orange melting moments 104
florentines 100
lemon shortbread shapes 98
quick chocolate walnut fudge 101

celebration menu

Whether for a mid-winter dinner or a birthday celebration, the following menu is guaranteed to be a winner!

Creamy Tomato and Basil Soup (page 41)
✿
Roast Pork Loin with Leek and Pistachio Stuffing (page 65)
✿
Roasted Root Vegetables (page 84)
✿
Ginger Sesame Beans (page 82)
✿
Rustic Rhubarb and Apple Tarts (page 94)

Prepare Ahead
- Make the soup the day before.
- Make the stuffing for the pork loin the day before.

On the Day
- Stuff pork loin and cook.
- Prepare and cook vegetables.
- Prepare tarts. Refrigerate and cook as the main course is served.

celebration menu (see above)

index